A Revisionist History of Loving Men

Lena Ziegler

Autofocus Books
Easton, Pennsylvania

Published by Autofocus Books
autofocusbooks.com

Memoir/Literature
ISBN: 978-1-957392-41-7
Library of Congress Control Number: 2025938860

Cover design by Amy Wheaton

A Revisionist History of Loving Men

For the girl I used to be,
the woman I am today,
and the many selves
I've been in between

Table of Contents

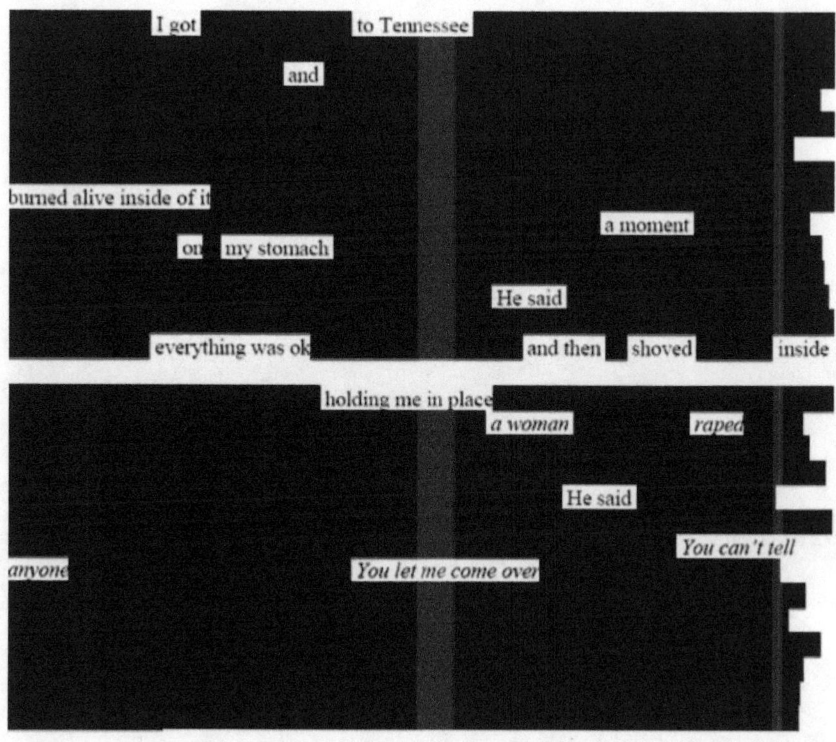
I got
to Tennessee
and
burned alive inside of it
a moment
on
my stomach
He said
everything was ok
and then
shoved
inside
holding me in place
a woman
raped
He said
You can't tell
anyone
You let me come over

PART ONE

Chapter 1

"Are you sure you don't want anything, hon?" The old diner waitress, missing a front tooth, blinked her tired eyes, reflecting the annoyance that if I didn't order anything, her only table would result in an even smaller than usual tip for a 4am Waffle House shift.

"Just coffee is fine." I smiled back and rolled the plain white mug between my palms. She stepped away, disbelieving, to submit the order. *Just coffee* for me, and an order of smothered and covered hash browns for the man sitting across the booth.

"I thought you said they had ice cream." I took a sip, gritty like mud.

"You want to leave?" he asked. He tore open a blue packet of sugar replacement and dumped it into his black coffee.

"No no, you stay, I'll leave," I said, straight-faced as ever. He smiled. White teeth, pinkish lips, red hair that stuck up and out like electrocution.

"You're sassy," he said. "I like it."

This was not the first time Jerry had called me sassy since our interaction began an hour and a half earlier on a dating website. He told me I was sassy nearly a dozen times that night. Had I been originally from Tennessee, like him, rather than a northeast transplant living there for less than a month, with an accent that instantly identified me as other, he likely would have considered my constant jabs and deadpan delivery bitchy rather than exotic and interesting. But something I had already discovered in my brief time living in a small city forty minutes south of Nashville was that the southern men I talked to found women from the northeast strangely appealing. The "smart" accent, whatever that meant, and preference for ball-busting over niceties, I'd been told, was "sexy." Or in this case, *sassy*.

My arrival at Waffle House a few minutes earlier, seated across from Jerry in his crumpled red flannel, thrown haphazardly over a black comic-book T-shirt like the very epitome of a twenty-six-year-old man living in his mother's basement, had little to do with my attraction to him and more to do with the fact that it was July 24th 2011, and I had spent the day before turning twenty three years old completely alone. I had moved to Tennessee from Northeast Pennsylvania on June 28th, one year exactly from the day I left my husband, Carl, and spent the following year hurting so profoundly most days that I found it difficult to keep from suffocating on my own impenetrable sorrow. I knew no one in Tennessee, had no job, no plans, and no prospects. I picked the state because I loved Americana music—blues, jazz, folk, alt-country, rockabilly—and dreamt I could redo all the mistakes of my still-young life by getting an apartment outside of Nashville and writing for a music magazine, because those jobs came easy, I thought, to eager, damaged, twenty-somethings with nothing to lose but sleep. This was my plan. To escape the torment of living a half hour drive from my ex-husband and the woman he had impregnated ten months into our separation, by melting into the sticky heat of a Tennessee summer where no one could even pretend to know me, or get close enough to hurt me.

But three weeks later, with my social interactions limited to a few job interviews, a handful of dates, and the beautiful and perpetually stoned roommate I found on Craigslist, who spent every weekend in Nashville with her tattoo artist boyfriend, I was already emotionally exhausted from being surrounded by strangers, day-in, day-out, with only a rare interaction dipping below the surface of superficial. When my birthday came and I realized it was the first one in my entire life I'd spend without my family, my friends, or Carl, I was filled with an ache unlike any other. I was truly alone in this strange city, in this strange state, as isolated as ever, the ink still fresh on my divorce papers, and the trauma from the experience of an addiction-riddled, abusive marriage coloring everything I did.

I spent the day trying to entertain myself. That morning, my mom had a cake delivered to my apartment, and I cried on the phone as I opened a package of gifts that she had sent a few days earlier. *It's too bad you have no one to eat that cake with,* I distinctly recall her telling me, the sting of her words unintentional. I hung up and washed my face, fixed my makeup, and headed to the car. I ventured to a state park nearly an hour away and laid on a tie-dyed blanket on the shore of a small lake. A hundred degrees outside, I stayed in the shade in my jeans, light blue tee shirt, and sunglasses. I laid back, resting my head on the fabric, and spread my long curly hair wildly around me, taking selfies on my flip phone. I thought I looked glamorous and grown up. I took a picture of my face, turned to the side, with blond wisps falling across my forehead, smiling softly. This is how you build a life, I thought. This is how you become okay.

After an hour, the magic wore off, and I was surrounded by children in floaties splashing along the shoreline while their parents took pictures, and young couples kissing and holding hands, their bikini bottoms and swimming trunks coated in fine layers of sand. There was a pressure building up inside of me, radiating through my legs, and pushing behind my eyes. I had to leave. Back in the car, I sobbed to Bob Dylan's *Blood on the Tracks,* not a "big girl" after all, and stopped at a liquor store. In my empty apartment, I drank straight from the two bottles of cheap wine. I finished both. I filled the remaining emptiness with pad thai and spring rolls, watched *Superbad* on repeat, and tried to connect with anyone I could on dating websites. A man who would later become a friend told me I was "unfairly pretty," the kind of fantastical comment often given by horny men on 2010s dating websites. We quipped about writing, music, and Seth Rogen, and I asked him, pleaded with him, to come over. It wasn't sex I was after, really. I wanted, and desperately needed, for someone, anyone, to look me in the eye on purpose.

With only an embarrassingly brief interaction leading up to my invitation, he, of course, declined, and I, of course, took it personally. I sobbed on the edge of my bed, wishing anyone in Tennessee knew I existed. Finally, around 3:30am, I took off my makeup, scrubbed smudged mascara, and dressed for bed. Just as I shut off the lights in my room, I heard the notification of a new message. I crept over to my desk and sat in the dark of the room, the blue glow of my laptop screen shining back at me. It was Jerry. After an hour of flirty rapport, Jerry asked if I'd like to get some ice cream. I told him no one around here has ice cream at 3:30 in the morning, and he said Waffle House did, that he was sure of it.

You'll have an ice cream and I'll have an early breakfast, he said. *I have work at 8am, so I promise I'm not expecting anything else.*

I figured the slight buzz in my system was faint enough, and I was lonely enough, to justify driving the 1.3 miles to Waffle House. We agreed to meet at 4am. Quickly, I reapplied makeup and threw on a fresh pair of jeans, and a cute top. I looked pretty good, I thought, for no sleep, a day of crying, and several pounds of Thai food and wine slushing inside of me.

When I arrived, I texted Jerry, who was a few minutes late. I'm not sure what I was expecting, but when he showed up, I was instantly disappointed. It's not that he was unattractive so much as that I knew upon seeing him, hearing his voice with a twang I didn't find charming, and smelling the lingering scent of cigarette smoke wafting from him, that he was not the man who could cure me of all my problems. As much as I wasn't looking for romance or even sex that night, some part of me still felt all suffering would someday be made better by the fatalistic love of a man in flannel, and sadly, this was not him.

About an hour and a half into our Waffle House "date," we stepped outside for Jerry to have a cigarette. I told him that cigarettes were disgusting and that I would stand by my car instead, all sassy-like. He told me I had a great ass. It was nearly 5:30am, and truckers were pulling into the parking lot, filling the booths, and crowding the restaurant beyond recognition.

"What do you want to do now?" he asked, taking a drag. I hesitated. I knew I didn't like this guy, but he had work at 8am and had said he wasn't expecting anything to happen between us. And I knew that I wasn't yet ready to be alone again.

"I don't know," I said.

"You said you live close, right?" he asked. "How about we go back to your place and take a nap." He was tired, he explained, from being up most of the night with insomnia. Plus, he lived twenty five minutes away, which is why he couldn't meet even sooner. "I work in Murfreesboro," he added, as a final clincher to his argument. "If I go back home, I'll just have to turn around and come right back here in a little bit."

I finally agreed that he could come over to take a nap. He followed me back to my apartment complex and building. I gave him a quick tour, and without missing a beat, he, as all men seemed to, zeroed in on the guitar in my bedroom and started playing, trying to explain chords and talking about all his experience with music. I was tired of him, frustrated by how little a stranger's presence did to temper the ache in me for some kind of connection, and reminded him he needed to work in a couple hours and should get some sleep.

"Lay down with me," he said, crawling onto my bed and kicking off his shoes. I stared at his body, sprawled across my bedspread as if it belonged there, and felt a twinge of annoyance. Still, I was exhausted too and didn't have much sass left in me to tell him to take the futon in the living room. I laid down next to him.

"Come here," he said, pulling me into him, his arm around me.

I rested my head and palm on his chest and stared out my bedroom window, the light of sunrise creeping in through the sheer curtains. He smelled of cheap body spray and cigarettes, and I was struck with the surreal reality that months of loneliness had culminated in this moment. Jerry was hardly the first guy I barely knew who would fall asleep in my apartment. During my separation from Carl, casual sex became a sport of catch and release. So much of my sadness in the last year had been doused with the temporary touch of lips, fingers, beards, and swelling want thrusted in me, I had begun to think of men solely as a means to an end—easy, reliable finds when it came to fulfilling a need for human connection on a short timetable. Plus, I loved sex and the tickle of uncertainty that came with undressing in front of someone for the first time and being desired, frantically, by them. There was a freedom that came with simply not caring who I had sex with, so long as I genuinely wanted to have sex with them, and they agreed to leave shortly after so that it would not be confused with something deeper than strangers in the night knowingly using each other. Often, however, the sex would end, we'd kiss or hug goodbye, and as the door clicked behind them, I'd fall into my bed, still lingering with the sweat and scent of another person, and cry myself to sleep, my body a broken, gaping void.

Moving to Tennessee had not changed these impulses in me, but shapeshifted them into something more intense. With my divorce officially underway, I not only wanted sex and connection to take my mind off things, but I also wanted the possibility of a romantic connection, or even love. Shortly before my move, I began talking to guys from my new town, not wanting to waste a minute, imagining the romance of moving to a new place and immediately falling in love. Upon arriving, I quickly met with one of them, but things fizzled shortly after. It turned out fresh new love wasn't as easy as tripping on synthetic marijuana from a nearby gas station and watching *Schindler's List* with a weird guy and his weird roommate. Still, I was hopeful.

As I searched for jobs, checked out local coffee shops, and explored Nashville, I kept up talking with one of the guys I was starting to fall for. His name was Eli, and he was a musician who, like me, was obsessed with Bob Dylan, and similarly had a talent for witty banter. Plus, he was cute, tall, and had a head of curly black hair that I found strangely sexy. The weekend before my birthday, he asked if he could come over after work, and I let him. He showed up with the kind of confidence, charisma, and chaotic energy I knew I could fall desperately into love with if I wasn't careful. Zeroing in on my guitar, Eli picked it up and tuned it carefully, pulling a metal slide out of his pocket, and slipping it down his ring finger. He talked about Robert Johnson, B.B. King, and Son House, while playing licks of the blues music he learned to play by ear growing up in southern Alabama. He was an incredible guitarist, sweeping through aching, tragic sounds I'd never heard come from a guitar before, or at least not in person. We talked about the space-time continuum, and he mused over the mathematical equations in stardust, the galaxy, the probability of all things everywhere happening. I listened to him play, inching toward him, longing for him to see how painfully drawn I was to him.

But we spent the night talking instead, and the longer we talked, the more enamored I grew. Finally, after seven hours, we crawled into my bed, exhausted, and he climbed on top of me, the leather strap of his necklace dangling above my chest. And he kissed me. Long and hard, minty, and my body nearly collapsed in on itself for all the riotous desire coursing through it. It felt like I was dissolving through him, disappearing into the haze of magic he brought into my life that night, now fumbling with the top button of my jeans, trying to pull them down. I pressed my hands against his chest and pushed him back, our lips separating for the first time.

"Not yet," I whispered, hot-breathed and uncertain. Why was I stopping this?

"I want you so bad," he whispered back in his 'bama drawl. We kissed again.

"Not tonight," I said. I pushed him up, and we stared at each other. He said my eyes were beautiful. I pulled him back into me, my fingers knotting through his hair as I kissed him again.

"Please don't make me beg," he whispered, his lips traveling from my mouth to my neck, kissing down my chest. I felt the blood rush through me—the energy of his magnetism, so intoxicating—except, I liked this guy. And the realization hit me, in all its misogynistic, puritanical glory, that men don't fall in love with girls they fuck on the first date. And I wanted this guy to fall in love with me, or at the very least, to see me again.

"Not tonight," I repeated, softly. He came back up to look at me. "Are you sure?" he asked, breathless, and I nodded. We were both smiling, but I could tell he was a bit frustrated. He nodded, kissed my forehead, and rolled to my side.

"Come here," he said, pulling me into him. We kissed one more time and he put his arms around me. We fell asleep, and in the morning he woke up, kissed me goodbye, and promised to text me later to make plans for the following weekend. We shared the same birthday and talked about how fun it would be to spend it together. I was elated.

But he never did call, never texted, and a week later, I was distraught with loneliness, resting my head on the chest of a man I didn't want, didn't even like, in the same spot I had been a week before, convincing myself I was inching toward something like love. Jerry didn't talk like Eli, or smell like him, play guitar like him, or turn me on like him. But he was there just the same, and we were falling asleep together anyway.

Moments passed, and I turned to roll onto my other side to fall asleep. Jerry stirred awake and pulled me in to kiss me. His mouth was dry and tasted like ash. My lips responded but just barely, feeling chapped against his. I pulled back. "I'm tired," I said.

"Just a little more?" he asked, and without hesitation, kissed me again, one hand on the back of my head to hold me in place. I wanted to wet my lips, to do something to make it feel slightly better. Then he pulled his hand from my head and thrust it, abruptly, between my legs, feverishly unbuttoning my jeans. I pushed him back.

"I don't want to, not right now," I said, meaning it. This was not the hot-and-heavy connection I had with Eli, when all that stopped me was a desire for him to not lose interest. I really didn't want Jerry to touch me that way, and with my lack of response, I thought it was obvious. "Okay okay," he said, his hands up, slightly defensive. "Can we just kiss?"

I didn't want to kiss him. It was unpleasant and did nothing for me. But I told him he could kiss me. I thought, I can get through kissing. Kissing a few more minutes wouldn't kill me, and it might spare him some embarrassment. So he kissed me again, and I tried to muster a physical reaction to his touch, searching deep inside for the want I wanted to feel. But I felt nothing except his dry lips smacking into mine, and his hand now slipping inside of my jeans, his fingers now inside of my underwear, and then, quickly, inside of me.

"Stop," I said as he kissed my neck. "Seriously, not right now." He pulled his hand back out, disappointed. "I just think you're sexy," he said.

"I'm sorry," I said. I felt genuinely guilty for disappointing him. I realized that he wanted this and had probably expected it, on some level, when I said he could come back for a nap. I was embarrassed for him and felt sorry I couldn't muster desire. I just wanted the situation to end and for him to leave me alone to sleep, wake up, and move on with my life.

"Can I just see your ass?" he asked, and I almost laughed. "Please?" he added.

I could tell, despite the playfulness in his eyes, that he wasn't kidding. I felt instantly uncomfortable, but at the same time, a little amused. Maybe if I gave him this, that would be enough, and he would stop. So, I rolled onto my stomach, laughing a little, embarrassed by what I was doing. "Here it is," I said, awkwardly inching my butt into the air. He grinned and rubbed his hand down my back and over my jeans, which had now fallen slightly down my hips, loose from unbuttoning. When his hand inched under them to rub across my underwear, I rolled back onto my side, shifting his palm to my hip instead. He kissed me, again, with a renewed force I might have liked if not for the taste of his mouth and the once seemingly harmless pestering that quickly morphed into an energy for sex that made me increasingly nervous. He pulled back to look at me, slipping his hand from my hip to unbutton his own jeans, pulling out his penis. Grabbing my wrist, he forced my hand down, wrapping my fingers around him and squeezing my hand shut. I didn't know what to do. He clutched my hand, moaning, and moved it up and down to stroke him, as if he knew I wouldn't do it myself. I couldn't believe what he was doing, but I didn't try to stop it. I'd had guys do things like this before, and even though it was unwanted and uncomfortable, I knew from experience that, as soon as he came, it would all be over, and he would leave me alone. But then he pulled his hand away, prompting me to reluctantly keep going on my own, and yanked my jeans down to grope my butt. I squirmed, trying to inch backward, away from him. But suddenly, with force, he rolled me back onto my stomach and got on his knees, climbing over me to straddle my body.

"What are you doing?" I said. I was frantic from the weight of his body on top of me and his hands and penis rubbing across my underwear.

"I just want to rub my dick against your ass," he said, placing his hands firmly in the middle of my upper back, crushing me tight against the mattress, and grinding his penis against my body. He was moaning, complimenting the curves of my body, telling me how badly he wanted me. I became angry and confused, suddenly realizing I couldn't push him off of me, but still believing he would stop, maybe to ejaculate on my underwear or in his hand, sure he wouldn't go any further when I obviously didn't want him to. He rubbed and moaned, slight pants escaping his lips, and I laid there silent, unsure what to do, trying not to think too directly about how little control I seemed to have over what was happening to me. With one hand still pressed firmly against my back, his fingertips folded beneath the elastic band of my underwear, and he pulled them down, quickly, so that finally he was in direct, skin-to-skin contact with my body.

"Stop it," I demanded. I tried to push myself up, panicking with the realization that I no longer believed he would, but his weight was crushing and unrelenting.

"Shh…it's okay," he whispered and rubbed his penis between the folds of my body.

"Don't—"

But suddenly he was there, his penis forced inside me, both of his hands now on my back, one inching up to grab my hair and pull it, my mind frantic with fear and confusion as the rhythm of his body pounded into mine, my face just barely raised enough so I could catch a breath as my chin pressed painfully into my pillow from his weight pressed painfully into me, and the realization of what he was doing convulsed through me, and I knew there was no stopping it with my hands, or my words, or my tears leaking out through my eyelashes, the immediate, inescapable truth that he was raping me, in my own bed, the spinning swirl of thoughts repeating through my mind: *he is raping you, you are being raped right now, you are now a rape victim, this is what you never thought would happen, he is raping you, you are being raped right now, you are a victim of this.*

I was crying now, fully, just barely repeating the words, stop, stop, and I'm not sure if it was the tears or suddenly my voice breaking through the fury of all his rabid thrusting, but he did, suddenly, stop. "What's wrong?" he asked, breathless.

"I told you to stop!" I choked out, barely able to speak.

"What?" he seemed genuinely confused. "I thought you wanted me to," he said, still straddling me, not yet pulling out.

"No, I didn't want to!" I said in tears. And with that, he pulled out and away from me, collapsing next to me on the bed. "What do you mean you didn't want to?" he asked, his voice raising in agitation, and possibly fear.

"I told you earlier," I said. "I didn't want to do anything. I sat up, relieved to be free of him, wiping away tears with the back of my hand.

"Then why were you making out with me and jacking me off?" He was frustrated, maybe even hurt. I didn't know what to say. Even in that moment, even after what he had just done, I somehow didn't want to embarrass him.

"I didn't do anything wrong," he said, adamantly. "I didn't do anything, Lena. You acted like you wanted to do it. I thought you wanted to," he paused, "I didn't rape you."

But, hadn't he? When had I indicated that I wanted to have sex? What had I done to make him believe that? My mind raced, trying to replay what just happened in my head, questioning what I had done, immediately doubting my own memory of what happened, thirty seconds after it had happened. I was silent, trying to quiet the noise inside, willing him to stop staring at me with his blue eyes, now so dark to me.

"You can't tell anyone about this," he said, suddenly, jarring me from my silent escape. "You can't tell anyone you invited me over here. I didn't do anything wrong. I didn't do anything. You can't tell someone I did something when I didn't."

He was scared. I could hear it in his voice. Scared, and possibly guilty, possibly aware, suddenly, of what he had actually done to me, the words he heard but ignored or shushed quiet, the hands that had pushed his own away, the complete lack of arousal evident throughout the body he had just violated. He was scared, aware, and waiting for me to say anything at all to comfort him in some way and assure him everything would be all right, that I would do as he asked and not tell anyone, that this would all just filter away from him, a bad night with a weird girl that cried during sex once.

I didn't know what to say, so I said I'm sorry.

In the living room, we sat on the futon and talked for a

while. He asked if I was okay and I said I was, that I was just a damaged girl, and I cried a lot. We talked about other things, but I don't remember what. I was raw, uncomfortable, restless inside of my skin. Something needed to happen to make things go back to before, when I was just a sassy girl, and he was just a boy in frumpy clothes who kept me company after a bad day. It was nearly 7am, and I was exhausted, my eyes aching. He was tired too, but still worried and restless in his own way. We went back to the bedroom to fall asleep, but then he kissed me again, rubbed his hands all over my body, and when he rolled me onto my stomach, pulled my underwear back down one more time, and climbed on top of my body, I told him to grab a condom first, and he did. He ripped it open, tossing the wrapper onto the floor next to my bed, rolled it on over his penis, and once again pushed himself inside of me. As he finished, I stared at the wrapper on the floor, not knowing why I had let this happen, the whole night, but most especially this last part, letting him fuck me less than an hour after he had raped me.

He rolled off of me, grunting and satisfied, this time not asking if I was okay, or even touching me for mutual pleasure. He fell asleep quickly, and I did too. Twenty minutes later, the alarm on his phone went off, and he sat at the edge of the bed, putting on his shoes. It was unspoken between us, the contract we had sealed by having sex. I couldn't recognize it at the time, but now I know that he needed to believe he hadn't raped me, and I needed to believe I hadn't been raped by him, despite everything within me that knew I had.

The sex didn't change anything. It didn't undo his body crushing mine into submission, his *shhh* over the sound of my dissent, or the swirl of acknowledgment rippling through me as he thrust selfishly in and out of my body, willfully ignoring what he knew was true. That I didn't want him. I didn't want him then, and I didn't want him when he tossed the condom wrapper onto the floor an hour later. Neither incident was truly sex. The first was rape, and the second was a desperate plea on both of our parts, especially mine, to pretend it wasn't. Because no one would choose to have sex with their rapist, I thought. No one who had truly been raped, anyway.

We didn't kiss or hug goodbye. I walked him to the door, and he said I'll text you, as many guys do. When he left, the apartment was quiet, and I was alone again with the gaping void of my body, not quite feeling like my own.

We didn't talk again. He never texted, thankfully, and I blocked him on the dating site. In the immediate aftermath, I went on pretending it never happened, remembering only the "consensual" ending to our time together. I told friends about the weird guy I met at Waffle House in the middle of the night, and they laughed about how random I was, and I laughed about how damaged I was, and I didn't tell a single person about what happened for another three and a half years. But throughout those three and a half years, every time I heard the word "rape" in casual conversation, in episodes of *Law & Order SVU*, in the statistic that 1 in 5 women are raped in their lifetime, I thought about Jerry, and cigarette ash, and what he had done to me. And I told myself it couldn't have been rape, knowing full well that's all it could ever have been.

CHAPTER 2

Growing up, I learned that rape exists as a constant looming threat to women, a violence of high possibility and likelihood that I would always need to keep myself safe from. When I was about fifteen, my grandfather informed me that if I was ever attacked, I should scream FIRE! at the top of my lungs, because then someone would listen. As he told me this, I tried to envision a situation in which I might have to do it. Immediately, I pictured myself getting pulled into a dark alley by a gun-wielding stranger, my clothes torn off as I was raped against a wall next to a dumpster, shouting with all of my strength FIRE! FIRE! as residents popped their heads out of multi-story apartment buildings, searching for signs of smoke. From what I understood, rape happened exclusively on shadowy streets in shady neighborhoods with strange men in ski masks, or at college parties with frat brothers slipping drugs into solo cups and assaulting unconscious girls on their roommates' beds.

While both violences certainly happen, with the college party scenario especially common, this particular understanding of rape has a significant influence on how rape victims interpret their own experiences, and how the greater culture at large responds to sexual violence narratives. When we are consistently shown a representative image of what rape is "supposed" to look like, by default we delegitimize any experience that falls outside of that description. This makes it difficult for women to recognize their own experience within the framework of "rape," with these sorts of popularized portrayals found to have a direct impact on how women name their own experience of sexual violence.[1] If it doesn't match the images, we think, it must not be rape. These portrayals also contribute to a more hostile response to rape victims who report assault that may not be seen as "that bad" compared to the absolute worst imaginable possibilities.

In the introduction to her aptly titled anthology, *Not That Bad: Dispatches from Rape Culture,* Roxane Gay resists this notion. She references her experience as a young teenager, when she was raped by a boy she liked and his friend group, and recounts her struggle to acknowledge the validity of her experience. She tells us, "For years, I fostered wildly unrealistic expectations of the kinds of experiences worthy of suffering, until very little was worthy of suffering…everything was terrible, but none of it was that bad." This hierarchy of female harm as result of rape is a common thread in narratives of sexual violence, institutional research, and even public conversations about rape. During the height of the #MeToo movement, it was common to hear even the most enlightened circles questioning why a woman didn't come forward sooner if her experience was so horrible, trying to establish a hierarchy of what was considered "bad enough" sexual behavior to ruin a man's career. As Elissa Bassist reflects in her own contribution to *Not That Bad,* so often for women "stifling trauma is just good manners."[2]

So, it is no wonder that the internalization of what constitutes "real" rape, and therefore legitimate trauma worthy of being voiced publicly impacts both a victim's ability to recognize her rape as valid (let alone reportable), and a public's ability to acknowledge all forms of sexual violence for what they are.

---

[1] Johnstone, Dusty. "A Listening Guide Analysis of Women's Experiences of Unacknowledged Rape." *Psychology of Women Quarterly,* vol. 40, no. 2, pg. 2016.

[2] Bassist, Elissa. "Why I Didn't Say No." *Not That Bad: Dispatches from Rape Culture,* edited by Roxane Gay, New York: Harper Collins, 2018, 324-339.

Though the two scenarios I spent my pre-rape life associating with rape (violent stranger rape and college party rape) are perhaps the most popular and widely accepted images of "legitimate" rape, there is also an unspoken effort to delegitimize even these through the cultural prominence of rape myths. Rape myths, which include such beliefs as "she asked for it," "he didn't mean to," "it wasn't really rape," and "she lied" are directly tied to the perceived validity of a victim's story.[3] In a 2016 study of college students' perception of the believability of rape victims' narratives, the findings overwhelmingly concluded that factors associated with rape myths, including the amount of alcohol a victim consumed, her prior sexual history, and her socioeconomic status, heavily factored into how "believable" her story was found to be, and how much empathy her story was met with. The study also found a direct connection between male rape myth acceptance and lack of empathy, with men showing greater compassion for perpetrators than victims.[4] Public empathy, then, for women who have experienced sexual violence is inconsistent at best. Which is to say, if rape is most often portrayed as one of these two images and even those are subject to disbelief, minimization, and a profound lack of empathy, instances of sexual violence that take place under different contexts have even less ground for understanding.

So, when as an adult I found myself in the presumed safety of my own bedroom, with a man I had soberly invited into my home, kissed, and sexually touched, who forced himself inside of me with my face buried in my pillow and the voice inside me screaming for release, I had no framework for understanding the situation as rape, and no wherewithal to shout FIRE! Even

---

[3] Rollero, Chiara, and Stefano Tartaglia. "The Effect of Sexism and Rape Myths on Victim Blame." *Sexuality & Culture,* vol. 23., no.1, pg. 1-11, 2018.

[4] Nason, Erica E., et al. "Prior Sexual Relationship History, Gender, and Sexual Attitudes Affect the Believability of a Hypothetical Sexual Assault Vignette." *Gender Issues*, vol. 36, pg. 319-338, 2019.

though by this time I understood that saying no and asking him to stop were clear indicators that I was not consenting, I still found so much fault in my own behavior that it felt unfair to hold him responsible instead of me. I spent the next three and a half years trying to internally unpack what had happened with Jerry and whether I had any right, whatsoever, to call it what I instinctively knew it was, bearing in mind that, during the incident itself, I was able to fully and thoroughly understand it at as such. I found myself thinking about the incident often, in rapid, cinematic flashes of light and shadow, of certainty and uncertainty, never lingering long enough to critically dissect it, but recalling it often enough to never move beyond it either. Sometime during those three and a half years, I whiplashed between total certainty that it was not rape, that memory and vulnerability had forced me to exaggerate the details, and the reluctant certainty that it was, but that I wanted to believe it was not. While I still wrestle with the former, I now accept the latter as evidence of growing up in a pervasive rape culture which normalizes sexual violence to such a degree that it can be difficult to distinguish it from regular sex.

The experience of being raped is many things, including highly confusing. While rape is most often framed as a frightening, sometimes violent, and frequently traumatizing experience that can forever inform the way an individual views their own body, sense of safety, worldview, self-worth, autonomy, relationships with other people, and sexuality, I believe the perplexing nature of bodily violation, how it is experienced and understood, is too often overlooked. The sheer confusion that being raped generates, not only about the incident itself—what to call it and how to respond to it—but what factors contribute to those things is a perspective rife with opportunity to further dissect how and why sexual assault is so normalized.

In recalling my rape in full, unwavering detail all these years later, after spending several years studying sexual violence, a few details stick out to me as noteworthy in understanding how gendered power imbalance around sexual autonomy, responsibility, and consent, informed both my and Jerry's behavior in addition to my own confusion around the incident to this day. Here's what I could glean from my own narrative:

As an early-twenties woman with extensive sexual experience before meeting Eli or Jerry, I implicitly understood the difference between sex I regretted or had for reasons aside from pure sexual desire, and sexual assault. In describing my use of sex as a coping mechanism during my divorce, I recognized that though sex did not always lead to positive emotional outcomes, the vast majority of sexual partners I had prior to meeting both of these men had engaged with me in enthusiastic, clearly defined sex acts. Though anecdotal, this pushes back against the all too common rape myth that women confuse "regrettable sex" with sexual assault. They don't. They inherently and instinctively know the difference.

Despite this, my sexual autonomy was in question before I ever even met Jerry, when during my interaction with Eli, I described my own struggle to circumvent the gendered sexual script that sleeping with a man would prevent him from forming a romantic interest in me. This reinforces a puritanical view of how sex is understood between men and women, and what my sexual responsibility as a woman entailed, including calculated chastity.

In a study exploring college students' understanding of consent, researchers interviewed college-aged men and women about their sexual consent behaviors, with the endorsement of sexual double standards as a major occurring theme.[5] One of these includes the belief that "*good* girls do not have sex," ev-

[5] Jozkowski, Kristen N., et al. "College Students' Sexual Consent Communication and Perceptions of Sexual Double Standards." *Perspectives on Sexual and Reproductive Health*, vol. 49, no. 4, 2017.

idenced in one male participant comparing finding a girlfriend with buying a new car: "'You don't want a lot of mileage on it'"... After college, he said, 'you want a wife and not a woman who's done all these people.'" Along these lines, both men and women endorsed the notion of women 'having standards.' The authors found that fourteen of the seventeen women interviewed detailed their experiences with avoiding or refusing sex to "demonstrate they have standards." ("Men stated that women who 'respect' themselves, and do not have sex with 'just anybody,' 'have standards,' whereas women who have sex with 'a lot' of men, or from whom it is easy to obtain sex, do not.") Seven women described regretting sex they had actually wanted to have for fear of looking like they didn't have standards. They go onto share that some male participants believe women resist sex to look good, and that men have to push past their refusal. The greater point to unpack here is that my sexual desire was not in this incident the primary factor contributing to my own decision-making about whether or not to have sex.

The experience of Eli respecting my sexual boundaries reaffirmed my belief that even in sexual scenarios involving virtual strangers who had great chemistry and desire for each other, it was safe to assume that voicing non-consent would result in the end of the sexual scenario. It seems obvious: sexual longing does not necessitate sex. It is the precursor, setting the stage for an invitation, which our partner may or may not accept, the choice theirs alone to make. This is how normal sex should work. We would not satisfy hunger with something inedible. By the same standard, we should not satisfy sexual desire with someone unwilling. This should, of course, be true in all cases.

As things grew physical with Jerry and I felt increasingly uncomfortable, I silenced myself to some degree for fear of "embarrassing" him by rejecting his touch more firmly. I reluctantly "consented" to kissing him, when I did not want to, in hopes that it would appease him while protecting his ego. Preoccupying ourselves with the fragile egos of men is something women are socialized to do from an early age; it can be difficult to pinpoint when exactly this becomes standard practice for most of us. Studies have found that by high school, most young women "give in" to unwanted sex largely for this reason—they don't want to embarrass, anger, or hurt anyone. In this way, young women's sexual communication mirrors how they are socialized to communicate in life with politeness, submissiveness, passivity, and a preoccupation with others' feelings at the forefront of their concern.[6] Their own feelings of comfort, desire, or even physical readiness is secondary. Additionally, college-aged men and women adhere to the belief that sex is a conquest and that women "owe" men sex as reward for his effort.[7]

My reaction was also embedded with an embodied knowledge that men sometimes force women into uncomfortable sexual situations that only end when the man reaches orgasm, mirroring a male-centric view of even consensual sex. As Jill Filipovic explains, "female sexuality is portrayed as passive, while male sexuality is aggressive. Sex itself is constructed around both the penis and male pleasure – male/female intercourse begins when a man penetrates a woman with his penis and ends when he ejaculates… sex is further painted as something men do to women, instead of a mutual act between two equally powerful actors."[8] When we are socialized to believe that sex starts with male desire—because good girls don't want it and bad girls aren't worthy of sex—and ends with a male orgasm—a few thrusts, a groan, and rolling over to sleep—the female in question be-

---

[6] Kitzinger, C, and H. Frith. "Just Say No? The Yes of Conversation Analysis in Developing a Feminist perspective on Sexual Refusal." *Discourse & Society*, vol. 10, no. 3, pg. 293-316, 1999.
[7] Jozkowski, et al.

comes a conduit through which male pleasure can be achieved, rather than an equal partner in the pursuit of mutual sexual satisfaction. If her enjoyment, or orgasm, is not pivotal to sex "ending," then why should her desire be necessary for it to begin?

When Jerry grew more forceful, I showed my disinterest in several ways including pushing him away, shifting physical positions, stating it directly (i.e. "I'm tired"), directly refusing (saying no and asking him to stop), and eventually even crying. Natalie K. Cook and Teri L. Messman-Moore classify resistance strategies in four categories: forceful physical resistance, non-forceful resistance, forceful verbal resistance, and non-forceful verbal resistance. Their research has found that the use of these direct refusal techniques leads to greater "rape acknowledgment" on the part of the victim. Rape acknowledgment is a term sexual violence researchers use to name the process through which a victim recognizes an assault as rape. When a woman engages in any of these refusal tactics, especially verbally voicing non-consent, and a man *still* rapes her, this directly leads to higher rates of rape acknowledgment.[9] The incident is less ambiguous in her mind. Which might explain why I immediately understood the experience as rape, but not my immediate distrust of my own memory.

As soon as Jerry stopped and we began discussing what had happened, I began to question my own perception, wondering if I had misremembered the situation. This immediate self-doubt is blatantly reminiscent of how easy it is for women to internalize rape myths that question the credibility of anyone who accuses a man of sexual assault, including her own. Victim memory,

---

[8] Filipovic, Jill. "Offensive Feminism: The Conservative Gender Norms that Perpetuate Rape Culture, and How Feminists Can Fight Back." *Yes Means Yes: Visions of Female Sexual Power and a World Without Rape*, edited by Jaclyn Friedman and Jessica Valenti, New York: Seal Press, 2019, 13-27.

[9] Cook, Natalie K., and Teri L. Messman-Moore. "I Said No: The Impact of Voicing Non-Consent on Women's Perceptions of and Responses to Rape." *Violence Against Women*. Vol. 24, no. 5, pg. 507-527, 2018.

point of view, or understanding of what happened is constantly called into question in rape culture, signaling to a victim that even their own perception might be faulty if held up against one that could be more flattering to the man in question. On a more obvious note, this also recalls the notion of women as passive sexual actors who must defer to men for sexual understanding and direction.[10] So, Jerry vehemently denied that he had raped me and immediately directed me to not tell anyone about the incident, presumably out of fear of legal recourse. He was adamant about this, and I implicitly agreed. Ultimately, I apologized to Jerry, which not only served as an early indication that I would shoulder the burden of responsibility for what happened for years to come, but that I had again internalized victim-blaming narratives and responsibility for male sexual comfort above my own. I believed on some level that by having "consensual" sex after the incident, we were erasing the incident itself.

This engagement in "consensual" sex may also have stemmed from a place of wanting to reaffirm my own agency after it was taken from me. Voicing non-consent and still being raped often leads to greater psychological stress because it reinforces the total lack of agency, and power the victim had over what happened to her in that moment.[11] Therefore, women may make the instinctual decision to not voice non-consent in situations where they do not want to have sex, but do not believe they have the power to stop it, because they understand that becoming a rape victim is a trauma they do not want. The avoidance of explicitly saying no is built on the belief that a sexual assault is only rape if it takes place after a woman has *verbally* dissented,[12] lending to the idea that unwanted sex for women is unavoidable, so it is their responsibility to keep it from turn-

[10] Filipovic

[11] Cook and Messman-Moore

[12] Cook and Messman-Moore

ing into "rape." It is important to note that this does not actually mean a woman wasn't raped, but rather that women who are feeling too pressured or afraid to verbally dissent (in spite of, in some cases, other non-verbal refusal tactics) may be doing so as an act of psychological survival.

I would classify my decision to have unwanted "consensual" sex with Jerry as a form of psychological survival, as well as avoidance. I did not want it to be rape. I could not bear it. I had to make it better. I had to form a new narrative—one that would absolve him of guilt and me of victimhood. It didn't matter what was true. So, while the answer may now be obvious, asking myself today why I didn't report Jerry for raping me, my answer is the same as it was then.

I just couldn't.

While years later, with the backing of scholarship and academic theory, I am able to critically evaluate this experience for what it was, this does not change the fact that I still struggle with blaming myself for the incident happening in the first place, feeling uncomfortable openly using the word rape, and questioning if I was complicit because I did not hold him accountable in the moment. In their Burkean analysis of blame and guilt in cases of sexual assault, Sandra French and Sonya Brown found that when victims attempt to maintain agency after being attacked, they must then grapple with the belief that they contributed to their own victimization. However, if they attempt to blame the man, there is also guilt for feeling as if someone else is taking the "fall" for something that is automatically their own fault. They explain, "Either the survivor is at fault for having the wrong attitude towards her attacker and/or failing to prevent her rape, or she must come to terms with herself as an agent whose will is not the only force that can control her body."[13]

[13] French, Sandra L., and Sonya C. Brown. "It's All Your Fault: Kenneth Burke, Symbolic Action, and the Assigning of Guilt and Blame to Women." *Southern Communication Journal,*

I believed I made the mistake by allowing Jerry into my home, believed I "failed" at preventing my own rape, and then felt I contributed to my own victimization by having sex with him afterward, thus leaving me conflicted in how I would name the violation I experienced.

While these beliefs certainly stem from the internalized misogyny of rape myths, Filipovic writes that in a rape culture in which women are taught to live in constant fear of sexual violence, focusing on the victim's behavior reminds women that their behavior is ultimately what will either lead to or prevent rape:

> The focus on the victim's behavior, rather than the perpetrator's, sends the message that a woman must be eternally on guard, lest she bring sexual assault onto herself. The 'if only she had…' response to rape serves the valuable psychological purpose of allowing other women to temporarily escape that sense of endangerment. If we convince ourselves that we would never have done what she did, that her choices opened her up to assault and we would have behaved differently, then we can feel safe.

Both realities are disempowering, complicated, and confusing, making my ability to confidently recognize this experience as rape all the more difficult.

So, I couldn't report Jerry for raping me. *I just couldn't.*

Chapter 3

In the years leading up to this incident, I believed with marrow-level certainty that if I were ever raped, I would boldly, bruise-faced and bloody-lipped, report my assault to the authorities and not stop screaming for justice until it was handed to me thoroughly and dramatically in a courtroom, with my rapist dragged away in handcuffs, never to be seen again. This certainty underscored my every interaction with the idea of rape prior to experiencing it. Rape was violent, gruesome, unambiguous, and most often committed by strange, monstrous men, and rape victims were frustrating, foolish, and weak not to report it, the nuanced reasons as to why they might not report never made clear to me. In the same way in which women are blamed for their own assault, they are also blamed for the outcome of both reporting and not reporting their rape as part of the cyclical nature of a rape culture in which a woman choosing not to report is accused of being complicit not only in her own rape, but the inevitable rape of other women at the hands of her rapist, while simultaneously being told to be careful, because reporting a rape can ruin a man's life. In both cases, the responsibility remains with the victim to first avoid rape and, if she fails at that, to then report the rape, but only under the right circumstances.

While the general fear of ruining a man's life certainly comes into question (though is debatable given the egregiously low rates of criminal conviction), reporting rape is far more complicated than this, including the all too common (and all too valid) fear of not being believed.[1] But before reporting a rape, a woman must first accept that what happened to her was not only wrong, but criminal. Not only criminal, but assault. Not only assault, but rape. To understand a sexual assault as rape, the incident itself typically must reflect a certain cultural script of what rape "looks" and "feels" like. In fact, research has found that women are often only comfortable using the word "rape" when their experience is consistent with popularized depictions of rape, and even then may take over a year to do so.[2] This may be due in part to the fact that naming an experience as rape requires a willingness to recognize the man, the perpetrator in question, as a rapist. These two tasks—naming an experience rape and recognizing a man as a rapist—go hand in hand. While 'rape' connotates a certain expectation of experience, 'rapist' implies a degree of monstrous humanity reserved for only the sickest, worst of our world. In a 2012 article, Shannon O'Hara found that reports about rape overwhelmingly refer to perpetrators as "beast" and "pervert," distancing them from "normal men."[3] This is why some of the most fundamental reasons women do not report rape boil down to one word: context.

What do I mean when I say context? I mean, reliving an incident over and over, not sure how loudly you said no, or if you actually asked him to stop, or if you were even audible in your silent worry of how he would react if you said anything, at all, out loud. I mean violation, unwanted penetration, no gun to your head, no knife to your throat, no explicit threat to your life, but just the fear, the crippling fear of your body splayed out before a man who wants nothing more than to pretend it's

---

[1] Nason, et al.

[2] Harris, Kate Lockwood. "The Next Problem with No Name: The Politics and Pragmatics of the Word Rape." *Women's Studies in Communication,* vol. 34, no. 1, pg. 42-63, 2011.

[3] O'Hara, Shannon. "Monsters, Playboys, Virgins, and Whores: Rape Myths in News Media's Coverage of Sexual Violence." *Language and Literature: Journal of the Poetics and Linguistics Association,* vol. 21, no. 3, pg. 247-259, 2012.

just him and your body, and you aren't even there at all. I mean his friendship meaning more than his fingers in your underwear, or under your shirt when you fall asleep next to him on a stormy night, and you wake up too afraid to move, worried you'll embarrass him, while fearful he may not stop. I mean not wanting to hurt his feelings. I mean not crying in the shower afterward, not scrubbing your skin until it is raw and bleeding, not feeling any dirtier than you did before, but feeling less your own every time it happens, every day you walk through the world a woman. I mean kissing his forehead, meeting his family, baking him strawberry birthday cake, nursing his dreams in the heart of your hands, encouraging him, seeing him cry for the first time, screaming your favorite song together at the top of your lungs with the windows down and the heaviness of everything flitting away through the strands of your own hair, whipping wildly around you both. I mean every reason you let it go, every reason you pretend it didn't bother you, every time you tell yourself "guys are just like that," every time you said "I love you" loud enough for him to hear and he said it back loud enough for you to ache, I mean every way in which he is not a monster.

Context. The degree of violence, the level of your own resistance, the severity of your reaction to it, and the many ways in which you love and trust the men who hurt you.

Despite the prevalence of the stranger-rape image in how women are taught to protect themselves from rape, 51.1% of female rape victims report being raped by an intimate partner, and 40.8% by an acquaintance[4] with women "more likely to be victimized in their own homes or in the home of someone they know" than anywhere else.[5] The "stranger in the alley" scenario is not only statistically far less likely, but also dangerously func-

[4] National Sexual Violence Resource Center, 2018, https://www.nsvrc.org/statistics, Accessed July 7, 2020.

[5] Filipovic

tions to keep women from identifying the significance of sexual assault in their own trusting, often loving relationships, that take place in the safety of their own homes. This is evidenced clearly in research about heterosexual consent communication. The context of a loving friendship or romantic relationship makes it additionally difficult for a woman to advocate for herself, as she is less likely to voice resistance for fear of hurting the man's feelings.[6] So, if rape acknowledgment is more prevalent in women who voice non-consent, and women assaulted by friends and romantic partners generally avoid doing this, it is understandable that this is just one factor, of many, that contribute to a woman's inability to clearly understand what happened to her in these cases.

Victims are not the only ones who struggle to acknowledge relationally based assault as valid, punishable forms of sexual violence. Nason et al. explain:

> Rape cases involving a victim and perpetrator who knew each other are less likely to be reported, and, if reported, are less likely to result in arrest, prosecution, and conviction than rapes involving a stranger. Women who have been assaulted by an acquaintance or an intimate partner also are less likely to seek medical care than women who have been assaulted by a stranger. Furthermore, individuals convicted of raping a stranger receive longer sentences than those who were convicted of raping an acquaintance when the degree of force reported during the assault was taken into account. Finally, lab research has demonstrated that when the relationship between the victim and perpetrator is depicted as being more intimate, as compared to less intimate, participants rated the rape as less severe and the victim as being more responsible and recommend a more lenient sentence.

If statistically 91.1% of rapes are performed by an acquaintance or intimate partner, this serves as a further reminder that most rape cases are not taken seriously. In her exploration of

[6] Cook and Messman-Moore

male sexual identity, *The Will to Change: Men, Masculinity, and Love*, bell hooks addresses this lack of critical engagement with sexual violence:

> Underlying this assumption [that men have to have sex] is the belief that if men are not sexually active, they will act out or go crazy... this is why rape – whether date rape, marital rape, or stranger rape – is still not deemed a serious crime...the assumption that 'he's gotta have it' underlies much of our culture's acceptance of male sexual violence.

Researchers refer to these gender norms and expectations of both male sexual needs, and romantic relationships between men and women as the 'cultural scaffolding' of rape. They include "wishing to maintain a relationship; feeling that a male partner was aroused to a point of no return; partner pressure – ranging from sweet-talking to explicit threats; fear of negative partner response..." and more, as normalized factors contributing to relationally based rape.[7] While victims of this sort of partner-based sexual violence may not know what to call these experiences of assault, scholars have been trying to come up with a proper "name" for it—gray rape, consensual unwanted sex[8] unjust sex[9] and unacknowledged rape[10] for starters. But for something that is supposed to be objective, that is legally, criminally, culturally inscribed as obvious, why is it so difficult to name an incident for what it truly is? And what are the factors that limit a victim's ability to name her rape, both internally, psychologically, linguistically, and rhetorically? Is it a limit on what we are willing to classify or call rape, or is it a limit on the language itself?

---

[7] Bay-Cheng, Laina Y., and Rebecca K. Eliseo-Arras. "The Making of Unwanted Sex: Gendered and Neoliberal Norms in College Women's Unwanted Sexual Experiences." *The Journal of Sex Research*, vol. 45, no. 4, pg. 386-397, 2008.

[8] Hakvåg, Hedda. "Does Yes Mean Yes? Exploring Sexual Coercion in Normative Sexuality." *Canadian Woman Studies*, vol. 28, no. 1, pg. 121-128, 2009.

[9] Cahill, Ann J. "Unjust Sex vs. Rape." *Hypatia*, vol. 31, no. 4, pg. 746-760, 2016.

[10] Johnstone

Despite everything working against me, the self-blame, the "imperfect" rape scenario of inviting a man over, kissing him, and having sex with him even after he assaulted me, I was still eventually able to name what Jerry did to me as rape. During conference presentations and in conversations with community partners, I have spoken these words out loud and told perfect strangers that I was raped—sometimes confident calling it what it is, other times through an uncomfortable lump in my throat, past the whisper within telling me I'm still the one to blame. It took years of personal turmoil and self-searching to name this incident rape, and even though that didn't result in me reporting the incident to anyone, turning myself into another nameless statistic, I believe the result of this was something far more profound.

The action of acknowledging this rape, naming it for what it was, was an important and necessary step for me to begin identifying other incidents from my life as sexually violent. Incidents that I had always, for some reason, brushed off as, if not acceptable then normal, simply because they happened with men I loved and trusted, rather than strangers like Jerry. Incidents that would leave deep, permanent marks on my sense of self, my ability to experience intimacy, and my overall sense of safety in the world.

Three and a half years after Jerry raped me the morning after my twenty-third birthday, I was able to call it by its name, openly and out loud, for the first time ever while sitting in a car, in a dark parking lot, with a man I had just met and would soon fall in love with. He was the first person I would ever talk to about my rape and the last person who would ever sexually violate me so horribly. I would feel the need years later to explore the uncertainty of what he did to me in a book-length project, seeking answers to the permanent damage he left behind in his wake, wanting desperately to understand why the trauma of forced, unwanted sex in a relationship does not seem to have a name that fits, or a word with the same powerful linguistic energy as 'rape' to describe it. He was the first person who made me see that Jerry was not the only person who had raped me and would not be the last. He was the impetus for my realization that three out of four of my most serious relationships, including my marriage to Carl, included sexual violations and violences I still do not know how to name, while also including strawberry birthday cake, singing at the top of my lungs, and exchanging *I love you* with heartbreaking tenderness.

In her foreword to the second edition of *Yes Means Yes: Visions of Female Sexual Power and a World Without Rape,* comedian Margaret Cho starts by writing, "For too long we've been shamed for being sexual, and we've been denied the language to describe our experiences." This, in my view, is the great hypocrisy of how our culture responds to sexual violence, and all the indication we need that there is still so much work to be done to understand it.

What I did not know when I began this work was how revisiting my body as a site of memory, where pain still lingers, and truth still exists somewhere deep in the folds of my need to forget, is how both the literal and not so literal damage to that body would disrupt the very process of working to understand it. In the months leading up to beginning this book, it became clear to me that the challenge of writing my stories as if they are only about sexual violence is that context is a necessary component to the narrative.

The context *is* the violence.

Revisiting the experiences seeded deep within me with a recognition of the contexts that spurred them into being, still present in every sexual interaction I have to this day and facing the simultaneous truth of both how much and how little I have survived, has reawakened an unrest within me I have long attempted to ignore, or cover up with productivity. I must acknowledge, now, that I am neither detached, nor objective in my understanding of sexual violence. Instead, I come to this work equipped with the embodied understanding of how it feels to have my love weaponized, to be shackled by shame, and to crave certainty of experience deep in my bones. I come to it as ready as I can be to pour out from within a profound relief and sorrow in knowing, I am not the only one, you are not the only one, and soon everyone else will know it too.

This is my revisionist history.

Chapter 4

Love is not supposed to hurt.

I first heard this Oprah-ism as a teenager, watching her talk show after school, as she spoke with victims of domestic violence. I still remember the cadence of her voice, the assertive, clear tone, and her confident declaration. The crowd applauded as Oprah stared directly into the eyes of millions of Americans and spoke this truth into being. But even then, as a high school junior surviving the persistent throes of emotional, romantic distress common to adolescence, I questioned the truth in this statement. Love is a burning thing, June Carter wrote, and Johnny Cash sang. It didn't seem possible that something as intense and all-consuming as L-O-V-E would not hurt, for just the challenge of harboring it inside of myself seemed an inscrutable fate to bear. Just existing while carrying the weight of such emotional attachment to someone else seemed detrimental to my long-term health, and yet, I couldn't help but crave it. If love didn't hurt, then what was I feeling in those early relationships, and why was everyone around me who claimed to be in love, actively suffering under the weight of it?

"In my twenties and early thirties I was confident I knew what love was all about," bell hooks writes in *All About Love: New Visions.* "Yet every time I 'fell in love' I found myself in pain." In this philosophical exploration of love and all its foundations and forms, hooks addresses the very belief I held onto that called into question whether Oprah was right about love. Is love ever able to exist without pain? Can it exist without hurt?

Though hooks is known for many things beyond this, including her intersectionality, pedagogy, and style and form of scholarship, for me, hooks is most remarkable for her commitment to dissecting and understanding love in a culture that fundamentally misunderstands and appropriates it for worldly gain. As with so many things in life, hooks identifies our early exposure to "love" as the guiding force behind how we experience love throughout the remainder of our lives. She writes:

> Learning faulty definitions of love when we are quite young makes it difficult to be loving as we grow older… We are not born knowing how to love anyone, either ourselves, or somebody else. However, we are born able to respond to care. As we grow we can give and receive attention, affection, and joy. Whether we learn how to love ourselves and others will depend on the presence of a loving environment.

For hooks, childhood abuse and neglect cemented her perspective on how to give and receive love. She describes an upbringing with parents who gave and withdrew affection as punishment, and physically abused her, and her siblings as the dysfunctional relational dynamic that followed her through her most serious romantic partnerships. Care was always to be earned, affection was never to be assumed, and the action of love was forever one-sided.

Though I am not here to blame my parents for my own struggles, at least not in this book, I can't talk about my own relationships without first recognizing that the splintering of my family, and the first-hand witnessing of a love turned toxic can only do so much to prepare a child for healthy relationships. I understand that there are layers to everything and that a million different simultaneous truths that can co-exist and contradict each other, especially when it comes to relationships. This has only become more evident throughout my life, as I've sought the answers to my own most burning questions about the nature of love. Questions that go beyond "should love hurt" and bleed over into the territory of "how much should love hurt" and "how much is too much hurt." So I don't draw this out to blame my parents, but rather to blame an early breakage for the cracks it left in the foundation, the fragmental knowledge of what it means to love and to be loved, remaining unclear to me throughout much of my adult life.

Throughout my childhood, romantic love had only looked like one thing. Through screaming, fighting, cruelty, and betrayal, I watched my parents' love disintegrate around me, their marriage dissolving much before I was even born, then ripping straight down the middle as soon as I was old enough to process the meaning of family. Their pain radiated around and through me, frightening me into submission, my siblings and I huddled together crying as their voices rose, and furniture was flipped and thrown. Storming out, slamming doors, a plant thrown at the wall and shattering against it into a million terracotta pieces. My mother on the floor in despair, each one of us rushing toward her, arms out, swallowing our fear and pain for the sake of comforting her. This was love in its rawest form: my parents driven to rage, and us children burying our own pain out of concern for theirs. For years, I used both of these lessons as reference points for the madness love can drive people to, proof of how intense love is supposed to be and feel. For how normal it is to hurt through love and how volatile love can sometimes be.

When after fifteen years of marriage my parents divorced and my mother quickly remarried, this was proof to me that love is destiny driven, despite the struggle to find it. Barry is my soul mate, she used to say, though now her memory denies it. A soul mate, a twin flame, a figment of romantic imagination—for years, I used this as a reference point, Barry coming into our lives with unapologetic hostility and open dislike for all of us—me, ten, my sister thirteen, and my brother fifteen years old.

For years, we all held onto the hope that as Oprah, or Dr. Phil, or some other daytime talk show host had said, it takes seven years for a blended family to truly blend. Seven years, half of a childhood, to wait for a family to finally start working, all clinging to the one core belief that it will get better.

But blending was not a possibility. As bell hooks explains in *All About Love*, there are men who are raised with a firm interest and investment in being loved, with little concern for giving love. This was Barry. For my mother's purposes, a man who she could pour endless energy and love into, without receiving it back. For my purposes, a stepfather who I could pour endless desperation for loving acceptance and acknowledgment into, with only cold disinterest, and hostile contempt in return. But as I learned to make myself quiet and small in his presence, this became another reference point for love. No matter how unhappy or unloving, no matter how dissatisfied, ignored, or neglected, it will get better.

Though my father moved on and into his own new marriage with my supportive and well-intended stepmother, his physical absence from my home, and the constant sparring between he and my mother throughout my childhood left me in a constant state of anxiety. After the divorce, my siblings and I became the currency, the power exchanged every other weekend, the bargaining chip for regaining balance after the destabilizing of divorce. I do not mean this in any reductive way, as I can only imagine the deep pain my parents were in as they experienced the ache for their children whenever we were gone. But the weight of guilt that pervaded my every phone call with my father for why I wasn't visiting more, and every conversation with my mother as I tentatively asked if I could spend more of Christmas vacation with my father, led to the conclusion that I was the primary source of pain in their lives, and any advocating on behalf of my own needs would just complicate the matter further.

These family dynamics are of course only one component of how we learn to love. Still, according to sex therapist Dr. Emily Nagoski in *Come As You Are,* attachment theory suggests "kids who are securely attached to their adult caregivers will, as adults, most likely attach securely to their romantic partners, and kids who are insecurely attached to their adult caregivers will, as adults, most likely attach insecurely to their romantic partners." Attachment styles, Nagoski explains, are the ways in which we connect to those in our lives, including family members, friends, and romantic partners. While half of American adults are believed to have secure, healthy attachment styles, the other half struggle with either anxious or avoidant attachment, both characterized by unhealthy relational impulses which make healthy bonds difficult to foster and open a person up for discontent and even abuse.

But it would be a long time before any understanding of my own attachment style, or even critical evaluation of my childhood, and gendered power dynamics, would become clear to me in dissecting the many reasons why relationships in my life followed unique, yet similar, patterns of abuse, distrust, and toxicity. As I grew into an adult, my child-then-teen heart explored love in its own child-then-teen way. Teen dramas, pop music, and *The Notebook,* all repackaged the same system of what it means to love. The Dawson and Joey "soulmates at fifteen" saga shoved down 90s kids throats (despite her infinitely better, less toxic options), Britney Spears singing "I was born to make you happy," on her first album at sixteen years old, Allie and Noah slapping each other in passionate angst, and me at twelve years old kissing my Joshua Jackson poster before bed, praying I'd grow up to look just like a teen idol, and practicing my first kiss on the back of my hand, like every girl has done since the beginning of time. These are all ways I internalized and reflected the pop culture I was consuming. The idea that love can drive people to madness, which I originally came to understand from my family dynamic, was reinforced in the media all around me. The near religious belief that I had in the idea of soul mates, understanding that no matter how toxic, or unhealthy something was, whether it was 'destined to be' was all that mattered in the end. These messages were, and still are, both exciting and inescapable.

As popular culture continues to expand to include not only movies, TV, magazines, pop music, and music videos, but social media as well, research about its impact on adolescents is increasing. Given the wide array of factors that impact an individual's understanding of romantic relationships, it is difficult to pinpoint exactly how heavy an effect popular culture has on early perceptions of relationships. However, studies show that when it comes to romance, pop culture consistently reinforces gender stereotypes, including the hyper-sexualization of women, the sexual dominance of men, and strong adherence of gender roles in romantic relationships.[1] This is even greater among African-American adolescents, as media targeted to Black audiences shows an even stronger prevalence for gender-based power as a normal part of relationships between men and women.[2] This knowledge begs the question: is media the cause of such subscription to gender roles, or simply a reflection of what has always been there?

Milena Popova, in her book *Sexual Consent* writes, "Our ideas of what is and is not romantic can shape our behavior in ways that limit our agency." If we believe angst is romantic, or

---

[1] Bogt, T.F.M., et al. "Shake it Baby, Shake It": Media Preferences, Sexual Attitudes, and Gender Stereotypes Among Adolescents." *Sex Roles*. Vol. 63, no. 11-12, pg. 844-859, 2010.

[2] Kulkarni, Shanti J., et al. "'I feel like…their relationship is based on the media': Relationship Between Media Representation and Adolescents' Relationship Knowledge and Expectations." *The Journal of Primary Prevention*, 40, 545-560, 2019.

if we buy into the notion that love is by nature both hard and earned, we may go into relationships ready and willing to ignore whatever red flags are wildly waving directly in our faces, begging to be noticed. As I grew older, my understanding of love could be whittled down to the few "truths" I held onto when it came to relationships: love can be volatile, frightening, and madness-inducing; it can be cold, hostile, and guilt-inducing; but it will get better and, in the meantime, all that matters is finding a soul mate, becoming worthy of their love, and fulfilling my purpose in life of pleasing them. Also, Oprah doesn't know what she's talking about.

What I failed to realize at the time was that what Oprah really meant was that someone you love should never intentionally hurt you and call it love. And while hurt in love may be incidental, it also should not be a necessary component to the system of love in the first place. A love that excuses, or worse, relies on hurt is not love at all, but something much darker. This is the truth I would spend the first three decades of my life trying to learn, while consistently confronted with relationships that would tell me otherwise.

CHAPTER 5

I first met Carl in 2007, when I was an eighteen year old virgin, and not proud of it, first year college student eager to meet a man who would want me as much as I wanted to be wanted by him. Carl was twenty four, an employee of the university I attended, funny in a hopeful stand-up comic kind of way, and significantly more experienced than me in all things sex and dating. We met by chance when I filled in for another student representative at a meeting Carl was also attending. Afterward, he followed me down the long staircase in the student union building, calling after me. I stopped and waited for him to catch up. At 6'4 and 350 pounds, Carl towered over me, the body of a former football player, with the warm, friendly smile of a twenty-something man trying to flirt with a girl. We chatted for a few minutes then parted ways. Later, he would tell me, and anyone who would listen, that sitting across from me in that meeting, all he could think was that this is my future wife, this is the girl I'm going to marry. It was love at first sight, he'd say, with a romantic certainty I have spent the years since trying to keep from perverting into entitlement. Once we were married, I would often reflect on this, wondering what exactly Carl had in mind when he saw me as his 'future wife,' and what expectations he held in his heart that I would later fail to live up to. But at the time, this was the ultimate romantic notion. A joy that fit my fantasy of soulmates and happy endings.

Still, it took a few months for Carl to convince me to go out with him. It's not that I wasn't interested; I was eighteen and he was twenty four, which made him seem ancient and me feel hopelessly naïve. He also didn't fit the fantasy I had about meeting boys at college. I imagined falling into a devastating affair with some gangly, bearded boy with an unironic passion for poetry and a dark side only to be cured by the shimmering brightness of love I would bring to him, the manic pixie dream girl he had waited for all twenty years of life. Not a grown man, with early glitters of silver in his sideburns, who didn't have a literary bone in his body. But it occurred to me that the sexual and romantic attention Carl was giving me might not always be available to me, a girl with stretch marks, hereditary chubbiness, and a deeply embedded belief that if I wasn't married with children by twenty three like my mother had been, it'd probably never happen. So, we spent time connecting, chatting through AOL instant messenger and poking each other on Facebook—the 'swipe right' of 2007. Finally, after months of pursuit, I agreed to go on a date with him. Five weeks later, we had sex—my first time—in a hotel room three miles from my parents' house.

In many ways, Carl was a great boyfriend. Though it's hard to remember now, over a decade after our divorce, all the specific reasons I fell in love with him, what I do know is that he was mostly kind to me, supportive, and made me feel sexy and beautiful all the time, despite my many insecurities. He was fun, happy, a beautiful dreamer coming up with plans for what life would be like when we were older and married, with a home of bright-eyed children. He'd go on about how endlessly happy we would be together, the kind of house we would buy, the careers we both might have, the breed of puppy we'd bring home for our kids, a highly anticipated surprise. Carl had an unparalleled love for dogs, and every time he saw one, he smiled. Not a quiet smile, like he was embarrassed to be boundlessly excited about something, in the way so many men in our culture are taught to be, but a big wide grin, like a little kid bubbling with unrelenting joy. This is one of the things I remember, so clearly to this day, loving about him. Plus, our sex life was beyond anything I could have hoped for. Carl cared deeply about my enjoyment, always making sure I was satisfied, wanting to try new things, and explore anything I craved. We would spend as much time as possible in bed together, touching, sweating, collapsing into each other, then repeating.

On weekends, I would visit him at his parents' house where he lived in his high school bedroom, a disappointing reality he explained away by the cost of living in the area, and spotty employment history (shortly after we started dating, he was fired from the job at my university, only explaining why with a simple "she was a bitch," in reference to the boss he struggled to respect). Each morning, his mother made us chocolate chip pancakes, and while Carl watched football with his father, his mom and I would talk for hours about the missed opportunities of her life—the journalism career she never had, the independence she never found, having gotten married in her early twenties, and immediately starting a family of four boys and no girls. Carl's father, a gruff Vietnam vet whose pain and rage permeated through every interaction he had with his family, seemed to make life miserable, with the brutality of his insults and verbal abuse directed at Carl's mother increasing in severity with every beer she handed him. Afterward, we'd go upstairs, and I would cry to Carl, who never seemed to know what I was talking about.

"It's like she is a slave to him; her entire life is about making him happy and he never is."

"She likes it," Carl would say. "Taking care of a family of boys – she's not unhappy."

But her world scared me. I imagined a life like hers, starting out so hopeful, wanting to make a difference, to write my way into existence, but instead meeting a man I thought was beautiful, falling in love and getting married, with the reality of my sacrifice heavy in every subsequent year of my life, feeling my spirit and humanity squashed out of me as I was actively ignored, or told to shut up and cook, by a family that didn't seem to know a single thing about me, who crushed beer cans in their fists, spit venom at each other—no one ever quite happy unless they were watching football. So whenever, in my urgency at nineteen to spend time with my boyfriend and not his mother, I grew tired of the hours I spent talking with her, I reminded myself that from what I could tell, my visits were the only time she got to talk to anyone who was interested in her as a human being and not as a servant to be talked down to.

I knew Carl had a problem with drinking when we got married. Amid all the good in our relationship, there were moments of pain. Nights working late in my dorm, writing papers and studying, then a phone call interrupting the silence, and suddenly Carl slurring through the speaker, his voice lazy, speaking in cursive, his tongue too fat with liquor to stay inside the lines. He called me a whore, a slut, a dirty bitch, a cunt, and I cried not understanding why. Attending a party in South Philadelphia with his work buddies egging him on, watching him get so wasted he couldn't remember what hotel we were staying in, and I found my way home, alone at 2am, heard him stumble in at dawn with a six-pack in hand, ready to drink some more. Watching David Letterman at his parent's house, Carl drunk on vodka straight from the bottle, telling me he would fuck me no matter what I said, only stopping when his parents came home. No matter what happened, the next day he'd beg for forgiveness, and claim not to remember what he said or what he did. He'd send me flowers, bring me gifts, beg me to forget that he was a monster when he drank, but still loved me more than anything, deep inside where the alcohol couldn't reach. After a year of this, I told him if he didn't stop drinking, we were done forever. So, he told me it would stop, and one day it did. He was no longer drinking and was back to being the man I loved, with the goofy smile reserved for dogs.

When we got married in August 2009, I had just turned twenty one. It had been a year and a half since the last incident, and I really believed he was better. We finally moved in together into an apartment, bright with tall windows and a yellow kitchen that made me feel like a real adult woman. A *wife*, but in a good way, I thought. On the outside, we were adorable young newlyweds. Our landlords, an older married couple allowed us to move in without any credit to speak of, and half a security deposit.

"I just have a good feeling about you two," the wife said. "And I'm a good judge of character."

But on the honeymoon, it was clear that Carl wasn't done drinking. He snuck liquor onto our cruise ship in a thin plastic bag, like an IV drip buried in his swimming trunks and polo shirts. One night, after he screamed at me, called me names, and kicked me out of our suite, I sat on the tropical print carpet in the hallway, my eyes red with tears and cheeks pink from the Bermuda sun, and took a picture of myself on the digital camera I received as a wedding present only a few days earlier. In the picture, it was clear I had been crying, the skin around my eyes translucent and puffy with sadness, my hair pulled back in a messy ponytail, unbrushed and knotted from chlorine. I'm not sure why I took the picture, what prompted me to think this was a moment worth recording. But as I stared at the close-up image of my face, with its sad frown formed from quivering lips, glow-ing back at me, I remember thinking about how incredibly long a human life could be, and how terribly young I still was.

Months passed and the situation only got worse. I worked long hours at a local nonprofit, planning events and raising money for a cause I knew nothing about, but it drained me so much that it was hard to wake up each day. Carl struggled to hold a job, getting drunk most nights of the week, and quickly blowing through the money we got from our wedding. I never knew a human body could hold so much alcohol and still survive. No one in my family drank, even socially, except for my stepfather, and he was a couple-beers-a-night kind of guy, not a serious drinker. But Carl in his bigness, in his habit, could drink an entire bottle of vodka in one sitting, and still stand up, still look me in the eye, and tell me he was going to kill me, without a second thought, before chasing me into the bathroom where I would lock myself away to hide from his rage until he passed out on the couch, covered in his own vomit, or shit, waiting for me to clean him up. The pattern was always the same. Either Carl was already incoherent, catatonic in his own drunken stupor when I got home from work, or he was perched on the edge of a brilliant violence waiting to erupt from somewhere inside of him where love didn't exist, and I was only a woman-body standing before him, waiting for him to hurt me.

I had grown up being told that physical abuse was a thing to be walked away from. Any kind of a "strong woman" doesn't stay with a man who slaps her, pushes her, or threatens to force her face into a frying pan of hot oil if she doesn't make his dinner right. "Strong women" walk away, or at least tell someone else it's happening, so that they may help them get the courage to leave. But this is not the reality of abuse, or even of love.

My motivations for staying were complicated. I didn't want anyone to know Carl was an alcoholic. I didn't want them to think anything bad about him. I wanted them to see him as I did—a charismatic, warm, funny man who was always good for a laugh and goofy conversation, always at his happiest when he was making someone smile, who loved me and wanted to be a father. And I didn't want them to think anything bad about me. I wanted them to see me as I knew they did—a strong, assertive, silly, driven young woman of twenty one with all of her dreams ahead of her and the talent and ambition to achieve them.

So, when Christmas came and we traveled to my mother's house to spend the night, my first time sleeping with my new husband in my old bedroom, no one in my life knew Carl had a drinking problem. No one knew he was still unemployed, that I was going broke paying his bills and mine, and that I spent most nights the last five months sobbing, locking myself away from him, or crouched on the kitchen floor, cleaning up his mess and praying he'd stop hurting me.

Besides, there was still some good between us. On nights he wasn't drinking, I was too grateful to see him sober to fight about all the times he wasn't, so we would watch movies, cuddled on the couch and kissing like we were happy. We'd go to open mics, and I'd watch him do standup, proud of how everyone in the audience seemed to love him. We picked out a Christmas tree together and made up songs, singing back and forth in the car when we drove around in the ice and slush of the city where we lived. Somehow, in my all my faith and hopefulness, I still believed it was going to get better, and there was no reason to tell anyone otherwise.

It was nearly midnight on Christmas Eve and my family had all gone to bed, still as excited for Christmas morning as we were when I was a child. Carl and I lay close on an old futon mattress in my old bedroom, watching a VHS tape of *A Christmas Story* again. About halfway through the movie, I started to fall asleep, and he whispered for me to keep sleeping; he was just moving to my great-grandmother's chair on the other side of the bedroom to get more comfortable.

"I can't sleep," he said.

When I woke a couple of hours later, stirred by the snowy sound of the TV still on after the movie had ended, it appeared that he had fallen asleep in the chair. Kicking at him playfully, I told him to join me on the mattress. His eyes lifted slowly, hazy and hard.

"What?" he said, loudly, his tongue slumped over the curve of his bottom lip, the slight glint of drool on his chin reflecting in the TV light.

My stomach shifted and settled into panic with the realization that he was drunk on Christmas Eve, in my parents' house, and no one even knew he was an alcoholic. Instantly, the pieces of my life that I had tried so hard to compartmentalize were coming together, and the narrative of my marriage that I had run myself ragged trying to control was slipping from my grasp, soon to unravel in a humiliating, public display of drunkenness and abuse I could no longer deny. My body flooded with fear.

"What?" He said again, louder.

I tried to quiet him, but he grew belligerent in his volume and aggression, pushing himself up to stand and lumbering over to the mattress. He fell on top of me, vibrating the floorboards of the old wooden house and sending a tremble of sound through the entire upstairs. Terror grew thick in my chest—what would happen if they woke up? If they all found out that this man they loved, who I loved, must have snuck alcohol in his overnight bag and waited for me to fall asleep before guzzling it down? In all my excitement about Christmas, and spending time in the safety of my mother's home surrounded by my family, it had never occurred to me that this might happen. Why hadn't it occurred to me? Why hadn't I prepared for this, checked his bag before we left, or broken the tradition of spending the night on Christmas Eve in case of this? How could I have let this happen?

His body shifted on top of mine, his weight crushing me into place. The sickly sweet scent of vodka spilled from his mouth as he told me he was going to fuck me. Though I was furious, shaking with worry that any moment my mother would fling open the door and discover the truth about my life, I tried to be gentle with Carl. I giggled something: *not right now, babe,* or, maybe, *not in my parent's house,* and I smiled somehow, as if strategic flirtation could save me from the situation or expedite its ending. But the more I resisted, the more impatient he grew. His fingers fumbled with the elastic waist of my bed shorts, slipped beneath my underwear, and thrust himself inside of me. I can't remember if it hurt, or if I told him to stop. I was assessing the situation—the danger of pushing his heavy body away from me and how he would no doubt react, screaming, thumping, punching his fists into plaster, or maybe into me. It would terrify my family. It would ruin Christmas. It would reveal him to everyone as the non-functioning, abusive alcoholic husband he was, and me as the weak-willed woman who stood by him.

I don't remember how much he really kissed me, just that there was slobber that tasted toxic. Maybe I kissed him back, or maybe I just turned my head to the side and stared at the snow, still crunchy white on the TV, and cried. Keeping my shit together while a man hurt me, not letting on how much, or in how many different ways. I only know that I was crying, and he was inside of me; I couldn't move, and there was nothing I could do to stop him.

The next morning, I greeted my family with all the appropriate holiday glee. I went through my day, opening presents, laughing, smiling, taking pictures, eating too many pancakes and cookies, and never addressed what happened, not with Carl, not with anyone. This incident remained a secret of my life, until now, because the shame surrounding this violation and the want for vocabulary to understand it still overwhelms me when I let myself revisit it. Plus, in the immediate afterward, my focus was not on myself, it was on him. Would he stop drinking? Would our marriage survive his addiction? Would he die young, his body flooded with toxicity, leaving me alone to rebuild my life?

When we separated the following summer, I began writing my way through the pain in long, swirly poems and free writes. I didn't expect this incident to surface, but it did—repeated proof of the moments I kept reliving in my body with any thought of another man touching me, whenever I walked past the room where it happened, while visiting my mother who, incidentally, was going through a divorce from my stepfather at the exact same time.

Shortly after our separation, I turned twenty two and agreed to spend the day with Carl. We ate at our favorite restaurant, and it was good to see his eyes, clear and warm, his smile genuine but tentative as he touched my fingers and kissed my hand. He asked if I would come back to the apartment that I had moved out of only a month prior. I told him I couldn't; it would be too painful. "Please," he begged me. "You're my wife."

We got a room at the Days Inn next to the gas station, across from the building where I worked at one point during our marriage. As we rode the elevator to the second floor, I felt queasy. Inside the room, he climbed on top of me and kissed me, gentle and kind. I cried softly but told him it was okay for him to continue. He lifted my dress and pushed inside, fucking me hard immediately. My quiet cries quickly turned into deep sobs at the reality of his touch, his body ripping pleasure from mine. He stopped and held my face, kissed my cheeks, and asked me what was wrong.

Chapter 6

Recalling the intricacies of a relationship so many years after its formal end is a strange experience. These recollections playback like cinema in flashes of light and sound, with anxiety rising inside as I watch, unable to change the outcome, certain I could not, even if I wanted to. It's taken years to stop blaming myself for things that I had no control over, despite the ever-present narrative inside *if only I hadn't…* that haunts so many of us when recalling the heartbreaks of our lives. It's taken even longer for me to recognize that Carl's addiction wasn't the only problem in our relationship, and hardly the only reason for our divorce.

To further dissect my own narrative of how our relationship started and ended, and all that happened in between, I want to identify a few key points:

When I met Carl at eighteen, I was already weighted down with the fear of how and when I would find love, overly concerned with the role my weight and age played in my validity as a romantic prospect. My value as a woman, and therefore my currency in seeking what I wanted in a partner and belief that I would find it, was grounded in my perceived sex appeal, invariably rooted in misogyny. In "How Do You Fuck a Fat Woman," cultural commentator Kate Harding explores the impact that thin-centric beauty standards have on the perceived attractiveness and sexual value of overweight women. She writes, "Women's first – if not only – job is to be attractive to men. Never mind straight women who have other priorities or queer women who don't want men. If you were born with a vagina, your primary obligation from the onset of adolescence and well into adulthood will be to make yourself pretty for heterosexual men's pleasure."[1] This assumption underlies every quasi-sexual, possibly romantic interaction women have. But for fat women, it can disrupt their sense of self-worth to a debilitating degree, altering their perception of the type of relationship they deserve or have access to. In sharing abusive comments posted by readers of hers and other fat-feminist blogs, she positions fatness as an excuse for dehumanization, and justification for rape with the old adage "you fat whores would be lucky to even get raped by someone."

Carl's own adherence to gender roles was remarkably present in not only his family dynamic, where he assumed his mother was happy and satisfied in fulfilling her 'wifely duties' despite a verbally abusive home environment, but also in his problems with female authority figures (i.e. his "bitch" boss). While all of this bothered me at the time, the relative normalcy of both forms of sexism made them feel more like immaturity than red flags for a relationship. Still, the reinforcement of traditional gender roles directly correlates with rates of relationship dissatisfaction, abuse, and sexual violence, with researchers finding that men who subscribe to "traditional masculinity" and endorse "traditional gender roles" are more likely to view women as sexual objects. In Rita Cantillon Seabrook's 2017 book *Alpha Alpha Alpha Male: Relations Among Fraternity Members, Traditional Masculine Gender Roles and Sexual Violence,* she studies the relationship between traditional masculine gender roles and acceptance of sexual violence among fraternity members utilizing the precarious manhood thesis, which posits that manhood

[1] Harding, Kate. "How Do You Fuck a Fat Woman?" *Yes Means Yes: Visions of Female Sexual Power and a World Without Rape,* edited by Jaclyn Friedman and Jessica Valenti, New York: Seal Press, 2019. 67-76.

is a status earned by performing traditional masculinity, and lost when not behaving 'manly' enough. This theory stems from hegemonic masculinity which requires, "being powerful, dominant, having several sexual partners, objectifying women, and avoiding any action that could be seen as non-heterosexual," while it "reinforces the gender hierarchy of subordinating women." Seabrook's study ultimately confirmed that the acceptance of sexual violence among fraternity members could be attributed, at least in part, to strong endorsement of traditional gender roles and masculine norms, which reinforce the view of women as sexual objects. In fact, studies have found that the largest demographic factors in men who sexually objectify women, and are likely to assault, rape, or coerce, is their association with religion and political conservatism, both of which correlate with the endorsement of traditional gender roles.[2] As a politically conservative individual, raised in a Catholic household that enforced gender roles, with family dynamics reflective of misogynistic views toward his mother, it is really no surprise my relationship with Carl was so troubled.

Early in the relationship, there were clear instances of abuse, and the cycle of abuse in both sexual, and non-sexual ways. The cycle of abuse can be most easily understood by referencing the Power and Control Wheel, developed by the Domestic Abuse Intervention Project and utilized by the National Domestic Violence Hotline to help identify abuse. The wheel identifies examples of physical, sexual, verbal, and emotional abuse, breaking down the cycle itself into four stages: tension building, incident, reconciliation, and calm. Each stage is distinctive, as the relational dynamic cycles from indirect to direct abuse, and apology to temporary bliss, before repeating. While experiences

---

[2] Ramsey, Laura R., and Tiffany Hoyt. "The Object of Desire: How Being Objectified Creates Sexual Pressure for Women in Heterosexual Relationships." *Psychology of Women Quarterly*, vol. 29, no. 2, 2014.

of abuse vary, abuse itself typically grows in frequency and severity over time.[3] While the verbal abuse was wrong to me, the pressure to have sex, and threats of forced sex did not register with me, at the time, as anything beyond what I should expect from a relationship. By the time we were married, and the scope of the abuse grew, my concern centered on Carl's addiction and my physical safety. However, sexually, I felt distinctly aware of the expectations that I would relent to his sexual advances out of obligation, if not out of desire itself, evidenced in my trip to the hotel with Carl, after his reminder that I was his wife. For many straight couples, the common assumption that being in a relationship is considered consent, prevails. This does not necessarily indicate that all of the sex in these relationships is nonconsensual, but rather that within relationships, consent is often seen not necessarily as a desire to have sex, but a willingness to. With the prevailing cultural belief that 'good girlfriends say yes' and 'once yes, always yes' consent in romantic relationships is less often negotiated and more often assumed.[4] Though in many cases this represents the ebb and flow of ongoing sexual dynamics in normal, healthy relationships, where partners become sexually familiar with one another to the point of not needing direct communication, it also represents those relationships in which this lack of explicit consent communication leads to pressure, coercion, abuse, and rape.

Abuse rarely exists in a vacuum where only one kind of abuse is present. The question comes with what kind of abuse do we consider valid and what kind do we pass off as a normal component of heterosexual relationships? Sex Role socialization theory suggests that "rape between dating partners should be

---

[3] Dubois-Maahs, Jessica. "Understanding the Cycle of Abuse." *Talk Space.* February 11, 2020. https://www.talkspace.com/blog/cycle-of-abuse-domestic-violence.

[4] Beres, Melanie Ann. "Rethinking the Concept of Consent for Anti-Sexual Violence Activism and Education." *Feminism & Psychology,* vol. 24, no. 3, 373-389, 2014.

viewed less as rape and more as part of normal sexual interactions, as forced intercourse supports the role of the male as the dominant party…as such, sex role socialization provides some form of explanation for why men are sexually aggressive and why the act of rape is normalized within society."[5] While most people would consider abuse a valid reason to end a relationship, if something is not viewed as abuse, but rather as a normal, albeit unpleasant, part of romantic relationships between men and women, how can a woman begin to identify that she deserves better?

During the Christmas Eve incident, I felt incapable of leaving the situation, protesting, or "avoiding" rape. This alone was a substantial contributing factor as to why I could not understand this situation as sexually violent. As discussed in earlier chapters, rape as we understand it, seems to designate a specific response of fleeing or fighting; i.e. directly avoiding rape, or attempting to avoid it, as the only acceptable responses to sexual assault that indicate non-consent. The idea that "freezing" might be a legitimate response to the threat of rape is one that is difficult to recognize, as it draws to the surface questions about what consent truly looks like if it does not always include a direct, or explicit refusal of sex. In *Come As You Are,* Emily Nagoski explains that to 'freeze' is a "life-threat stress response, activated when your brain decides you can't escape a stressor, nor can you fight it…survivors don't 'fight' because the threat is too immediate and inescapable; their bodies choose freeze because it's the stress response that maximizes the chances of staying alive." In my situation, my fear of Carl's previous abuse, and my family's presence, triggered my freeze stress response, which ultimately led to me blaming myself for the incident.

---

[5] Grubb, Amy, and Emily Turner. "Attribution of Blame in Rape Cases: A Review of the Impact of Rape Myth Acceptance, Gender Role Conformity, and Substance Use on Victim Blaming." *Aggression and Violent Behavior,* vol. 17, no. 5, 443-452. 2012.

The relationship between alcohol and sexual violence is statistically staggering. Some studies have found that up to 75% of perpetrators and over 50% of victims consumed alcohol before a rape took place.[6] More often than not, the presence of alcohol reinforces the misogynistic myth that women who drink voluntarily in the presence of men are putting themselves in danger. Rarely does conversation about a perpetrator's sobriety go beyond excusing his actions. There is a disarming inconsistency with the treatment of victims and perpetrators: "When exploring research relating to perpetrator intoxication, the literature reveals a counterintuitive double standard which renders intoxicated perpetrators of rape as less responsible for their actions than sober perpetrators. This is, of course, in stark contrast to the attributional effect observed with victim intoxication, whereby victims of rape who are intoxicated are held more responsible and more to blame for the rape."[7] This adds another layer to the context surrounding the Christmas Eve incident with Carl. While I was sober (and therefore a more 'believable' victim), Carl's inebriation made his violent behavior seem more excusable, as I could willfully deny that his true (sober) self would do the same thing.

The entirety of my relationship with Carl, the good and the bad, all form the complicated context for why the incident on Christmas Eve, as well as the other non-consensual moments from our relationship, made recognizing the validity of these experiences as sexual abuse difficult. My desire to protect Carl's reputation within my family and to maintain the relationship, along with my focus on other more pressing (i.e. less normalized) forms of abuse, made my ability to identify these experiences as problematic almost impossible. Additionally, the

---

[6] Grubb and Turner

[7] Grubb and Turner

assumption that a relationship status automatically presupposes consent, reinforced that my role as Carl's wife stripped me of my autonomy.

Finally, the context of the relationship, my complicated understanding of consent, and a lack of language that felt representative of my experience turned this incident into one I could not name, and therefore have kept almost entirely secret.

Until now.

CHAPTER 7

In *Against Our Will,* Susan Brownmiller writes, "To a woman the definition of rape is fairly simple." While I acknowledge the partial truth of this statement and its recognition that the experience of rape is most often a clearly felt violation of autonomy, I push back against the notion and myth that rape is defined simply for women or, by extension, easy for women to name. In fact, rape, along with many primarily female experiences, with its long history of being denied, excused, diminished, and questioned, is so complicated that the presumed simplicity of it, based on definition alone, is essentially false.

There is a long-held, complicated relationship between human experience and the acquisition of language to describe it. In *Man Made Language*, Dale Spender explains:

> In order to live in the world, we must name it. Names are essential for the construction of reality, for without a name it is difficult to accept the existence of an object, an event, a feeling. Naming is the means whereby we attempt to order and structure the chaos and flux of existence which would otherwise be an undifferentiated mass. By assigning names we impose a pattern and a meaning which allows us to manipulate the world.

Naming, as Spender describes it, is a necessary, fundamental component of all human experience. There can be no discourse until there is language to power it. This is perhaps easiest to understand in considering the vastness of human languages and which experiences are declared fit for naming. An example of this might be the French term "L'espirit d'escalier," which roughly translates in English to 'staircase wit,' meaning the feeling of coming up with the perfect response for a conversation, long after it has ended.[1] Words such as this are sometimes referred to as "untranslatable" words because, "above all, they appear to indicate the existence of a phenomenon that has been overlooked or undervalued in English-speaking cultures."[2] In these cases, culture dictates what sensations and experiences are worthy of naming. So, if one culture, for whatever reason, does not value an experience, or recognize it as part of its cultural identity, there may be no name for it, even if it is readily experienced by individuals within that culture every day. This, then, creates the lived experience, without the language to understand it, and thus the basis of this naming debacle.

So, what factors dictate whether an experience has a name? Spender would offer that human language has been constructed through a patriarchal framework specific to the human male experience above all else, leaving women's experiences on the periphery of available language. This has been referred to as a co-cultural group distinction:

> In patriarchal societies, women traditionally constitute a co-culture...a co-cultural paradigm posits that, in contexts where their experiences are marginalized, co-cultures participate in and negotiate their status within the dominant discourse by using particular communicative strategies. Co-cultures can be defined as pariah in respect to dominant social groups (468)... dominant groups have 'partial and perverse' views of reality, because to them the reality of marginalized groups is invisible.[3]

This co-cultural theory reinforces the necessity of names in understanding experience. For if there is no representation in lan-

---

[1] "19 Unique French Words You Need to Learn." *Optlingo.* Accessed October 28, 2020.

[2] Lomas, Tim. "The Magic of 'Untranslatable' Words." *Scientific American.* July 12, 2016.

[3] Burnett, Ann, et al. "Communicating/Muting Date Rape: A Co-Cultural Theoretical Analysis of Communication Factors Related to Rape Culture on a College Campus." *Journal of Applied Communication Research.* Vol. 37, no. 4. 465-485, 2009.

guage, the experience linguistically does not exist, despite the very real, lived moments that embody it. This is the basis of Ardener's Muted Group Theory, a feminist communication theory that explores how the experience of a disempowered population (women) is "muted" in the dominant (male) culture. As Wall explains,

> Women's voices trying to express women's experiences are rarely heard because they must be expressed in a language system not designed for their interests and concerns. Unable to symbolize their experiences in the male language, women take one or two routes: one path requires internalizing male reality – alienation; the other is being unable to speak at all – silence.[4]

The rhetorical impact of silence is perhaps best explored in Cheryl Glenn's *Unspoken: A Rhetoric of Silence.* While the text as a whole is an exploration of silence as a rhetorical action that can come from an empowered place or position of authority, she argues "the question is whether our use of silence is our choice (whether conscious or unconscious) or that of someone else." She explains that "silence goes unnoticed, (or, if noticed, then appreciated) in those whose words are not value," suggesting, for the purposes of this work, that women's silence on the issue of sexual violence—whether that be in not reporting assaults, and/or naming them as such—is reinforced by a culture that fundamentally does not value their words or experiences. Drawing back to muted group theory, Glenn says that without accurate language, women must "adapt, mediate, and subordinate" their ideas to fit within the dominant discourse. I see this lack of language as a fundamental factor contributing to the normalization of sexual violence in heterosexual relationships. If there is no fitting word to name these experiences, then there is no way to distinguish them as anything but normal.

But herein lies the problem: is it so difficult for women to

---

[4] Wall, Celia J., and Pat Gannon-Leary. "A Sentence Made by Men: Muted Group Theory Revisited." *European Journal of Women's Studies.* Vol 6, no. 1, 21-29, 1999

name their experiences as rape because the word itself is simply not appropriate, or inclusive of their nuanced experiences? Or, does the cultural dialogue around rape render it impossible for women to recognize their own experiences in the only word available to them? Is it the language itself, or is it the culture?

This may be another example of simultaneous truths. The word rape is loaded with meaning that goes far beyond its definition, complicating how and when it can be comfortably used by women who have experienced sexual violation. I have argued in regard to my own experiences, and those documented in sexual violence research, that context of a relationship and the gendered constructions of power that prescribe expectations of what constitutes 'normal' heterosexual sex, both contribute to the challenge of naming some experiences of non-consensual sex, rape. The rhetorical implications of the word rape, notably, that rape is always violent, committed by 'monsters,' and unambiguous in nature, can disrupt a victim's identification with the term to the point that it does not feel fitting. Therefore, rendering rape both an inaccurate term *and* an experientially unrelatable term.

The question is, who does this limitation of language truly serve? If language reflects the reality it creates, it does not exist separate of the cultures it functions within, but rather, it is constructed to reinforce the system it serves, adapting as necessary to understanding the human condition. If we believe, as Spender, Burnett, and Ardener offer, that women are a co-culture group, muted by the lack of available language, this limitation can only serve to reinforce the power structures of a patriarchal rape culture, which is upheld by adherence to traditional gender constructs, and directly benefits from the normalization of sexual violence as a regular part of that dynamic.

Whether the word rape is the problem may not actually matter in the end. On one hand, we have this word—rape—

that carries with it an embedded cultural meaning that can give it great power. On the other, this word is so charged with expectation, that its very simplistic definition keeps women from recognizing their own experiences in it, further silencing them. Spender argues that while a feminist impulse to develop new terms might make sense, there is still trouble to be found in this approach. "New names," she writes, "systematically subscribe to old beliefs, they are locked into principles that already exist, and there seems no way out of this even if those principles are inadequate or false." If this is true, where does that leave victims grappling with their own experiences, advocates fighting to dismantle rape culture, and educators hoping to further the public's understanding of sexual violence and consent?

In the first episode of her podcast *Unlocking Us,* Brené Brown speaks to relationship between power and advocacy:

> Sometimes we're afraid to name experiences or feelings because we think naming them gives them power...Let me dispel this myth now with 400,000 pieces of data in 20 years of research, when we name and own hard things, it does not give them power. It gives us power. And what do I mean by power? The best definition of power that I think exists in the world is from Martin Luther King Jr. Power is the ability to affect, change and achieve purpose. So, if we put it all together when we name and own hard things, it doesn't give the hard things power. It gives us the power to affect, change and achieve purpose.

Whether embracing the word rape, or fighting for new terminology all together, one thing is clear: not much can be done without naming. Which is why advocates, educators, and researchers from all disciplinary backgrounds, but especially those specializing in language, should take seriously the question: for however many women there are who claim the word assault and the word rape, how many exist that do not, and what might that tell us about the reality we have constructed?

Chapter 8

The first time I ever directly wrote about Carl was in a memoir class while completing my MFA. In an essay I facetiously titled "My Barbies Fucked Like Animals," I recounted my youthful attempts to learn about sex from peers, pop culture, and yes, Barbie. At only 750 words, the essay spanned from ages five to twenty three, boldly calling attention to my many awkward attempts to understand sex, without actually having to get too vulnerable in the process. I summed up my relationship with Carl like this:

I first had sex with Carl, who immediately after taking my virginity asked if I had ever tried Proactiv. We were married and divorced four years later.

This retelling of our story was intentionally vague, for a laugh. My professor circled it and wrote in green ink in the margins that this could be a micro-essay by itself. I loved that idea. Because for all it said about our relationship—a nod to my age, the length we were together, Carl's entitled remark about my appearance in such an intimate, vulnerable moment, and the implication that all of these things had anything at all to do with our divorce—there was so much it didn't say, and flat out got wrong about it. Incidentally, this essay was also the first time I ever wrote about sexual violence in any capacity, with the end of the essay flipping quickly from the humorous, light-hearted tone throughout to something darker:

I was 23. He had me on my stomach and I couldn't move. It was combat. He had a warhead missile. I had words he said he couldn't hear for the sound of himself exploding. I wet my pillow with streaks of mascara. He said I made him feel bad. I said I was sorry. The battle continued. He fell asleep beside me. I couldn't sleep at all.

A body lying on top of you so you can't move isn't sex, it's something else. But no one ever told me that. And that's something no one likes to talk about.

And that's how I ended it. A blunt confession in exactly one hundred words, told with judgment about how no one talks about the realities of rape, when we talk about sex.

Afterward, my professor came to me and told me he believed that I needed to expand the ending, that it was the center of gravity for the piece and I couldn't just trail off at the end without resolution. This is the same feedback I received from multiple editors in my attempt to publish the essay without revising it, believing instead that there was power in the unspoken, un-pressed subject of sexual violence in an essay about Barbie and sex education. While I do stand by the "less is more" approach in many cases, I recognize now that my reluctance to expand this scene had a lot more to do with my complete and total desire to not ever talk about this incident again, than to own up to the fact that maybe a first draft of something I wrote wasn't, in fact, perfect. After this, I would go on avoiding writing about sexual violence for as long as I possibly could—one year exactly—before returning to another memoir workshop, with the same professor, and having my world blown open by the course reading list, filled with books about rape, trauma, writing, and researching through the healing process. I would ultimately spend my final semester of my MFA working on one long, complicated essay about consent, critically confronting as much as possible within myself and my sexual history, without actually attending therapy, or healing at all from the incidents themselves. In the end, the essay did not make it into the final draft of my thesis, leaving the whole of my sexual trauma explored in it to only one hundred words in that Barbie essay.

That brief, snarky retelling of my relationship with Carl was one of the only mentions of him in my thesis as well, despite spending my first memoir workshop writing a thirty page essay braiding narrative about our divorce, my parent's divorce, Bob Dylan's *Blood on the Tracks* album, and the murder of a young man I attended college with who I didn't know personally, but whose death had rocked me to my core for reasons I still don't quite understand. So, years later, after our divorce and many attempts at blocking Carl from my life, he found my thesis published online and read the Barbies essay, and the short excerpt about the rape on my twentythird birthday. He texted me from a new phone number.

"I'm sorry this happened to you," he said. "I'll kick his ass."

The irony, I knew, was lost on Carl. I never addressed the incident on Christmas Eve, and he likely didn't remember it even happening. But the reality is that even if he did remember, it is unlikely he would remember it as it happened, or in the same way I remember it happening to me. Despite everything I know about sexual violence that tells me I did not give consent to Carl, that I actively did what I could to prevent it, that the physical threat of his body on top of mine, and that feeling that I was trapped with no option to refuse sex can only make it one thing, I don't feel comfortable calling it rape. It feels disingenuous to our whole relationship, which was riddled with toxicity and its own kind of violence, but which I never believed was an intentional kind of hurt. So, I took to calling it a violation—a word that feels right in many ways, but doesn't carry the weight or the imbedded cultural knowledge of what that looks like, or even means.

If I could talk to Carl about it today, I'm not sure that I

would. The last time we spoke, the summer of 2018, shortly after he had reached out about the Barbie essay he had read, he asked if I could ever see us together again. He promised me that he had changed, he was no longer a "monster," and that I had been nothing but a wonderful wife to him when we were married. I told him a partial truth, that I had forgiven him, but that I no longer thought about him at all, not sure which part was fiction. There was a crisp finality to our conversation, a revelation of pain that we both still felt, amidst an understanding that there was no longer any reason to talk, and that there hadn't been in years.

Our love had been an uneasy blend of purity and turmoil, of firsts and lasts. But the reality is that in all my reflection and time away from our marriage, one truth stands alone as powerful and telling as anything could be: In the span of two years and one month, our marriage came to a swift and brutal end, and a rape had nothing to do with why.

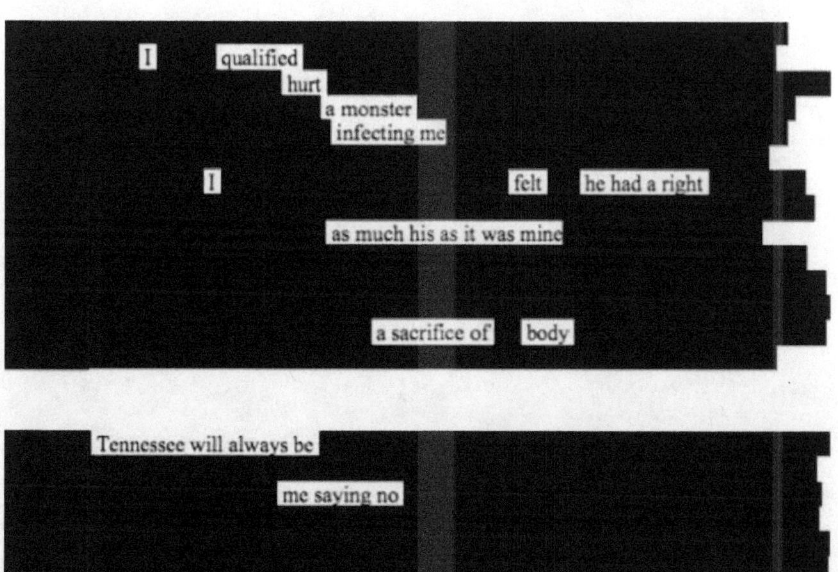
I
qualified
hurt
a monster
infecting me
I
felt
he had a right
as much his as it was mine
a sacrifice of
body
Tennessee will always be
me saying no

PART TWO

Chapter 9

"But even before fucking entered the ever-growing swell of my sexual lexicon, I never once referred to it as making love. Perhaps the making of love is simply an antiquated phrase built from an even more antiquated idea, hinged on naivety and hopefulness, as if love itself could be manufactured right along with the heat and friction of genitals colliding. Is there anything else quite as sad, or misleading, I began to wonder, as turning love into something physical, that could be broken, lost, fractured, forgotten? If we cannot force someone to actually love us, how then can we force someone to make love with us?" —Lena Ziegler, "Consent After Birth"

"We cannot capture in writing some 'real and actual' moment in our lives. We know that every event is shaped and interpreted such that we can only speak about 'how it seemed to me.' If we paid careful attention, we'd see that we construct fragments of our experience into stories or mini-narratives, excluding some features and emphasizing others, to organize and make sense of them. . .we tell ourselves our own personal histories by means of these self-narrated moments." —Candace Spigelman, *Personally Speaking: Experience as Evidence in Academic Discourse*

I met Shane in January 2015.

I don't have a way of talking about this yet.

Chapter 10

December 2017 – In therapy, I worry I'm talking too much. I apologize for talking too fast, for not being a good storyteller, for rambling on. The counselor is gentle, and he asks why I am here. I tell him I don't feel anything. I am muted. Even. Almost inhuman. On the phone with my mother, I had called this peace.

He asks me when this started.

#

For whatever reason, a memory sticks. My mother, brother, sister, and I eating stromboli at our favorite pizzeria thirty minutes from home in the city where I had been born nine years earlier, and where my mother now traveled to the YMCA every Wednesday night and weekend to burn off sadness while we visited my father. We did this every so often in the time between my father and Barry, the four of us bonding over the special treat of time together in a place free of melancholy. Most of our trips there do not resonate any kind of unique memory, each one blurring together into happy nostalgia for that short and special time.

But during one of these pizzeria visits, somehow, a conversation about rape arose, my mother asking us all, between bites of gooey mozzarella and greasy dough, *Who do you think a woman is most likely to be raped by, a stranger or a person they know?*

I answered immediately, as the youngest in the family, forever eager to prove to everyone how smart I was. *A stranger,*

I said, confidently. Of course, a stranger.

But my mother shook her head. *No,* she said. *Women are more often raped by someone they know.*

I don't remember a single thing about the before or after of this moment. It's as if it exists in its own mini universe, floating, detached, in the ether of my childhood memories, and the many ways I came to learn about life. I don't know how this came up (though I assume it was inspired by one of my mother's Women's Studies courses she had taken at a nearby university), or how my siblings responded, or what my mother said to explain what she meant. I just know that it didn't make sense to me. How could someone do that to someone they know? *Why* would they do that?

That being the violence unique to women, I thought at the time. That being the ugly ripping sound the word reminded me of. That question being the one I'd never stop asking. Why. Why. *Why.*

So, she said, *you have to be careful about who you know.*

#

Summertime 2017 – I moved to Ohio, my fourth state in four years, ready to start my PhD program in August. My best friend, Erin, visited me a week before school started, and we swam in Lake Erie, took sunshine-y pictures together, went to a bar and did karaoke. A group of guys invited us back to their house to smoke weed, and we agreed, buzzed by the obvious danger of it all. At their house, two of them played pool while we got high with the others, giggling inappropriately as they argued the ethics of nuclear war. Erin sat quietly, arm twisted overhead, twirling hair between her fingers, a hazy smile across her face. I kneeled in front of the coffee table, sharing my opinions about graduate school, death, and sex. As one of the guys attempted to sing the notes tattooed on Erin's foot, the other, Art, stroked my back, complimented me and asked me to check out the rest of the house. I eyed Erin, and we left shortly thereafter.

The next morning, one of the guys texted to tell me that Art was recently engaged, and I shouldn't get involved with him. This, I told Erin, was not surprising. If there was anything I had learned in the previous two and a half years, it's that relationships, marriage, and love meant nothing to men with a sexual agenda, which was, from what I could tell, pretty much all men.

It had become a joke in our friendship to laugh about the damage we did to ourselves, embracing our own wildness in the name of sexual freedom and being interesting. It had become a joke for me to name my last several months living in Kentucky "the summer of old men," a facetious title characterized by my regular involvement with significantly older, usually attached men, in situations that were both emotionally and physically dangerous. During most of that time, I felt unhinged, a wild animal unfurling, existing only in the ethereal space above my bed, watching myself perform. I showed up places, touched people, spent nights alone or next to men who didn't know me. I conceived of myself as something: a fantastical other, already ruined, imaginary, an empty, context-free fuck, hardly human, a figment of unreality.

I knew nothing except my body.

What Shane taught me to do with it.

#

December 2017 – I cry during the intake counseling appointment. It's the first time I have cried in months. I don't recall when I first noticed all this not crying I was doing, except that it started when I moved to Ohio.

After Erin left, school began. I struggled, so scared and desperate, earnest to the point of embarrassment. I told myself in Ohio, things would be different in my life. My focus would be on school, on writing, on finding a relationship worth something, on growing into someone deserving. I wanted abstinence—to find value in just existing. I was determined to put my summer, and the years leading up to it, behind me, let all my wildness dissolve into someone else's memory of me.

Two weeks into the semester, I went to a bar with a new friend. From across the room, a man spotted me, came to my side, bought me a drink. We smoked weed in the alley, talked about our PhD programs. He was tall and funny, and I sensed something sick about him in a way that intrigued me. Back inside, we sat in a booth with a group of mutual acquaintances. Under the table, he stroked my leg, pressed tight against me, whispered things.

On our first date the following week, he made a reservation, and we both dressed up. I felt like a proper lady. We had dinner, and I ate slowly and pretended to be dazzling. He drank craft beer and pretended to be a gentleman. On the way home, he asked me to come to his place to watch a movie. *Nothing will be happening,* I told him, and he smiled. *Of course not.*

Thirty minutes later, a movie about aliens, a bowl freshly burned, the two of us tangled in heat, and sickness swirling through me. Too dizzy, too affected –

I feel crazy right now…

You seem fine to me—

I knew nothing except my body, queasy and desiring, spinning and on fire.

The next morning, he dropped me off at my apartment and thanked me for a wonderful time. I smiled brightly, kissed his cheek, waved goodbye, and stepped inside my apartment, fell to the floor, and wept.

I tell the counselor, *I haven't cried since early September.*

#

When I used to kiss the back of my hand, I pretended it was someone who loved me back. This was well before I knew what it meant to love someone. There was a time when I thought sex would only exist where love was found. There was a time when I thought love and sex were intrinsically linked—twin threads spooled together, a perfect union of physicality and emotional depth, symbiotic by nature. In the context of true love, no sex was off limits. It became my fantasy to fulfill fantasy, my need to fulfill needs. It was an act of love to burrow deep into the furrows of another person's want and emerge bright and happy to provide the answer.

I was unprepared to learn that sometimes sex and love were incompatible, each willing to parasite off the other for survival.

#

December 2017 – It's cold in Ohio. The last day with walk-in hours at the counseling center. I fill out the forms and sit in the waiting room, staring at the jigsaw puzzle of two kittens playing with yarn. I wonder what it means to be a danger to yourself. The doctor greets me from ten feet away, and I smile, following him back to his office.

My body is shaking, on the edge of some great explosion. He asks me about my relationship with my parents, my siblings, food, drugs, and if I have ever experienced addiction. He doesn't ask about sex, if I have ever used it for self-harm, or to act out dangerously, or if I disassociate during it. This is not a question anyone asks during therapy intake. He asks about sexual violence, and I tell him, yes.

I don't trust anyone. I tell him, the world is dangerous and unsafe. Besides, I am ruined, broken. I'm afraid of men. I am afraid everywhere I go that I will see one man, in particular. I get flashes of him at the grocery store, walking across campus, stopped next to me in traffic. I see his car everywhere, I think. I see his fingers in other men's fingers and hear his voice when other men speak all gentle and patronizing. I hear his voice in my head, smell him in my apartment.

But he lives 450 miles away.

I apologize to the doctor.

I can only talk about Shane in fragments. I have tried for more, but I never met a language I trusted enough. How do any words, ever, hold enough?

Chapter 11

January 2015 – His body moved like liquid across the coffee shop, slinky in a way, like dancing. He spotted me first, but I pretended not to notice. When we met, his face was old to me. He ordered coffee at 10pm. He sat down across from me, and I closed my laptop.

I thought, *What am I doing here?*

I said, "I'm working on my novel."

#

In 2011, after filing for divorce, I moved to Tennessee, turned twenty three, and returned to Pennsylvania a few months later. I eventually found a place of my own in a nearby town, an apartment most recently rented by a heroin dealer who my new landlord told me broke his lease after getting a prison sentence. When I moved in, the entire apartment was littered with garbage, rotten food, and cigarette burns in the crumpled brown carpet. It was also, strangely, attached to a dentist's office, and sometimes, in the middle of the night, I heard drilling, and imagined a scenario in which the neighborhood dentist was a serial killer.

I worked at a donut and coffee shop and in the office of a local college. I got a third job as a hotel front desk worker and spent the little free time I had writing at a quirky coffee shop a short walk from my apartment. I bought crunchy bread at the bakery next door, spent money I didn't have at the health food store down the street, and a used vinyl record shop in nearby Scranton. I was piecing a life together, but I was alone with the tremors of the previous years, and the pained residue they left behind inside of me.

Over time, sex had become the one way to meet people my own age, and I had begun to think of it as my only social currency—the only way I could pivot would-be strangers into friends (with benefits), and sometimes short-lived boyfriends. Though years later I still believe much of the sex I had during this time was consensual, it often left me feeling empty and unseen. The divide between intimacy and sex was growing stark, with little crossover. There were those men I fucked and those men I loved. The former was much easier to find.

#

January 2015 – I'd gotten used to people asking about my novel, but not so used to people listening to me talk about it. But from the moment we met, Shane was consumed by me.

It's about two characters, I explained, nursing my own near empty cup of coffee. *A man and a woman, and about how everyone ultimately is using each other, whether for love, or sex, or friendship. It's supposed to show the nuance of relationships, how we are all capable of being the bad one, or the mean one, or the wrong one. How it's human to sometimes be cruel.*

He smiled at me, his long face lighting up with interest. There were wrinkles around his eyes, deep creases from a weathered life.

He asked, *Do you think there's anything that's unforgivable?*

#

I spent 2012-2013 in love with Jay, a man I referred to as my soul mate for many years after our breakup. Our relationship had been intimate and romantic; it felt like once in a lifetime. But after months and years of believing sex was the only way I could connect with another person, it was clear that sex was the one way Jay and I could not. Over the course of a year and a half together, we only attempted sex a handful of times, and rarely to either of our satisfaction. Jay couldn't exactly explain it to me—he wasn't asexual, he wasn't gay, but he just didn't want me. He tried his best to reassure me that this was a problem in all of his relationships, not just ours. But when I would cry about it, share how much I needed to feel that connection with him, he would mostly remind me how unimportant sex really was when you have something like we had. For as long as I could, I agreed with him.

In the moments leading to our breakup, he stood in our kitchen, carefully cutting a watermelon we had purchased at a farmer's market earlier in the week, which we had been excited to taste together. I watched his arms and back clench as he slid the long, clean knife through the thick peel of the fruit. I said it out loud, to his back and collapsed to the ground behind him. We spent hours sobbing, howling, crawling through the apartment to and away from one another, hurling pained words, begging forgiveness, begging for chances no longer available, pleading with one another for this to be easier.

Pulpy pink juice dribbled from the countertop, landing in a small puddle on the kitchen tiles. It felt like hours that I sat and watched it all fall away.

#

When Jay and I broke up, I felt destroyed in a way I didn't know possible. Though it had only been two years since my divorce was finalized, the wounds of my marriage to Carl still fresh enough to hurt, it somehow didn't compare to the pain of losing Jay. It was like a limb had been severed from my body. I cried checking guests in at the hotel, I cried on the weekly drive to my mother's house to do laundry. I cried ferociously multiple times, every day. The only time I wasn't crying, it seemed, was when I was having sex.

In many ways, Jack was everything a rebound should be. He was sexy in a dangerous way, while at the same time, someone I knew, under no circumstances, I would ever fall in love with. At the hotel, he delivered pizza nightly to guests staying in our various suites. Each time, he would linger at the front desk, joking, flirting. When Jay and I broke up, he told me that I was a sick woman for valuing sex more than I valued love. When Jack came along, with his attraction so blatant it bordered on objectification, I couldn't resist the feelings of validation this sprouted within me. After a year and a half with Jay, feeling unwanted and longing for some connection, Jack's consistent, aggressive pursuit of me was intoxicating.

Jack was unlike anyone else I had ever met. He was the product of a violent, broken upbringing, in and out of foster care, juvenile detention, and eventually jail. His pain was bred from a combination of childhood abuse and neglect, melded with struggles with mental illness, and an association with poverty he wore as a badge of honor. Like so many men who came before, he triggered within me the deep desire to transform him and his life with the power of my warmth, care, and affection. Jack was many things, most especially a bold, outgoing, intelligent, hilarious, goofy person, whose sheer mass in height and weight and propensity toward violence with other men, made him the kind of man destined to go through life as the one phone call someone would make whenever in trouble and needing someone ready to fight.

But, as so many women do, or at least as I have so often done with men who were clearly wrong for me, I searched for the depth in Jack and found a lightness shining through the black hole of pain that swallowed him and informed the decisions he made for how he lived his life. As strong as Jack presented himself to the world, I could see he was lost, and I wanted to help him find his way. I invited him into my life because at the time I believed attention was a valid substitute for love and respect, and that my capacity for love was best spent on the people who had no idea how to return it.

#

On our second date, Shane and I met at an upscale Italian Restaurant in Nashville. As we ordered, the waiter's eyes flicked from me to Shane and back again, the nature of our relationship a question apparent on his face as he talked politely through the options for vegetarian pasta. As the night progressed and we discussed both of our previous divorces and shared passion for literature, my concern for what other diners around us might be thinking of us there, together, shifted to a total and complete focus on Shane. Talking to Shane was like talking to a real adult man who still somehow saw me as an equal. He had perspective on life, decades of career experience in publishing, an adult son just a couple years younger than me attending law school in Knoxville. He had an MBA, was the editor of a major Christian music magazine, and had a kind of gentle, thoughtful demeanor I had never encountered before in anyone. Every conversation thus far had been wildly stimulating, but there in the candlelight, with the restaurant closing down around us, a deep warmth expanded inside of me as we spoke, his gaze unwaveringly fixed on mine.

Outside, we stood next to my car under the parking lot light and talked for another hour before agreeing it was too cold to not at least warm up the car. We sat in the front seats. An hour later I whispered, *I've never told anyone this.*

#

When I recall my relationship with Jack, which in total lasted about nine months, from fall 2013 to summer 2014, I mostly remember the good parts—hours spent belly-laughing together like children unable to catch their breath, cooking together in an apartment kitchen that was in no way up to code, playing my ukulele and singing songs together. But there was a darkness about our relationship that even now I am uncomfortable acknowledging, mostly because I still struggle holding him accountable for it.

As much as I grew to care for Jack, I didn't love him in the way I had loved other men.

And love meant too much to me to pretend otherwise. But Jack was consumed with desire for me to tell him that I loved him. He brought it up in casual conversation at any chance, and I'd always look sadly back at him, not sure what to say. For a lifetime, I prided myself on never breathing those three words to a man without full disclosure of what they truly meant to me.

One evening, in the lamplight of my apartment, I slid to the floor and knelt before him. I put my mouth around him and looked in his eyes. He followed my gaze, smiling, his hands in my hair directing my movement. But as he grew closer, he began to ask for something.

I want you to tell me you love me.

This was not the first time Jack had demanded that I tell him how I felt about him, but it was the first time he held my head in his hands, my voice muffled by his flesh pressing the back of my throat. A dread filled my chest, but I chuckled, trying to be playful and offset how uncomfortable he was making me. He persisted.

I pressed my hands on his thighs and pushed myself away from him. *You know how I feel about that,* I said, more serious. *I've told you, I can't say that until I'm ready.*

But Jack had spent his life believing brute force was the only reliable way to get what he wanted, and if my I love you was not to be freely given, it was something he felt entitled to take when and how he wanted. Clutching my hair, he forced my head down and his penis back into my mouth. *Say it,* he said. *Say you love me.*

Panic struck through my center as I realized I couldn't breathe. I slapped his thighs, the sign I had given other times we got rough together, a sign that told him to slow down and let me go. But he didn't let go and instead urged me further.

Say it now and this will all be over, he told me. He was smirking, enjoying himself with a sadistic grin. I shook my head, determined not to give into him. But with my nose pressed into his flesh and my eyes filling with tears, my body started to shake. My fingernails dug into his skin, and I tried to pull myself off of him.

But he held my head still.

Say it, he said, slowly. With our eyes locked, I watched his face turn dark. He was not going to let me go. He was going to force me to say it. I blinked back tears and tried to speak, but only a gurgle came out. He asked me again, and I tried, again, to say it. I said it over and over until the urgency of my fear and anger came through the muffled sound, and I articulated, as clearly as physically possible, *I love you.*

He laughed, letting me go, and I pushed myself off of him.

I knew it, he said, smirking.

When I pulled back, my lips dripped syrupy defeat. My body convulsed, breaking into sobs. I don't remember what I said to him, just that I screamed. My voice rang through the tiny apartment. I stood up, trembling as I rushed to the bathroom, pulling the door closed and locking myself inside. The mirror above the sink was speckled with water marks from shower condensation. I stared at my reflection. My eyes were red and blinking. I knew in that moment that something had been taken from me, but it took me years to figure out what that was.

#

When we first met, Shane said I owed it to both of us for me to give him a chance. Having only moved back to Tennessee from Pennsylvania six months earlier for a position in AmeriCorps, I could count on one hand the people I had social contact with each day. For the first several months of living in Clarksville, I was determined not to pursue sex casually with anyone, opting instead to pass the days with work, cooking dinner, watching *Chopped*, and going back to sleep. I spent my weekends writing at a local chain of evangelical coffee shops and reading on the steps of a nearby park, overlooking the Cumberland River. I joined a bowling league through the university where I was working and filled every Tuesday night with the habit of attending. Once again, my life was filled with an aching, impenetrable loneliness that I couldn't shake. I spent most days asking myself why I moved there at all, what was so bad about Pennsylvania, and what it was about Tennessee that kept drawing me back. I was now living an hour and a half from the town where I had been raped four years earlier. What exactly did I think I was escaping from?

#

Jack rapped his knuckles on the door and asked, Are you okay? I stared at my reflection, dewy black around my eyes. I stood crying. This was not a man who I loved, or ever intended on loving. He was not meant to be more than a body from which I could rebound, but he had told me he loved me a few weeks in, and I didn't run, so perhaps I should have expected this. Though our sex life had been adventurous, he knew that saying I love you was the one thing I wouldn't, and couldn't do, and he found a way to take that, still.

This was not the only time Jack would violate me in our relationship. Months later, while I was sleeping, he forced himself into a part of my body I had rarely allowed him to touch. I woke screaming, fighting away from him, and fleeing to the bathroom where I once again cried at my reflection in the mirror. This incident, especially, is hard for me to talk about. I have spent years doubting my own memory of what happened. Because I was sleeping, I have worked out a million different ideas about what might have happened instead—maybe he was just touching me, maybe he tried to penetrate me but didn't succeed, maybe I overreacted—but none of these ideas ever absolve him of guilt or morph it away from sexual violence.

Time passed, and these incidents built up a legacy inside of me, coloring my perception of my relationship with Jack, while at the same time feeling so normal; it was hard to pinpoint why exactly they bothered me. Was it how wrong they clearly were, or the fact that neither one led to me ending the relationship? Jack was claiming to be in love with me, introducing me to his mother on Easter, and crying in my arms, for the first time in front of anybody, about the shame he felt for being a fuck up. I didn't know how to hold someone who I saw as a victim of their own circumstances accountable. It would be years until I'd begin to understand how two things can be simultaneously true: 1) a person in pain is deserving of love and compassion, and 2) that doesn't mean I have to date them, forgive them, or tolerate abuse from them. The truth is that we never talked about either incident until 2017 when, during the height of the #MeToo resurgence, Jack reached out to ask me about our relationship. Until then, I buried the violation somewhere deep inside of me, swallowed the violence and made plans for my life that would take me far away from him and everyone else who had hurt me.

In summer 2014, I broke up with Jack by moving 900 miles away.

Six months later, I met Shane.

#

I said, *I've never told anyone this,* and Shane listened. I told him the story of Jerry raping me the morning after my 23rd birthday. When I finished, his eyes were wet, and he kissed my cheeks.

I said, *I never feel comfortable using that word, but any time someone says the word rape, I flash back to that moment.*

His fingers traced from my cheek, down my shoulder, and into my hand. He held it tightly. I said, I'm not sure if it was though. I wiped my tears away with my shirt sleeve. *I don't know if I'm allowed to use that word.*

You're allowed to use it, he said, kissing my hands. *Of course, you are. It happened to you. And it shouldn't have.*

The world was silent as he kissed me.

I just want to know you, Lena.

#

There are some men who, when they hear you have been raped, when they find out your body once existed as the site of another man's violence, imagine the ways they might participate in your history of violation. Such men want to plant the flag of their hard-pricked desire to make you remember them forever, long after you've lost your relevance to one another, in the threads of your sexual history. It is important to me that I remember Shane as he was—silent gunfire, a slow leak of poison, a violence threaded through everything. It is important that I remember his shift away from gentleness into something like ownership, when he first proposed that true vulnerability was handing yourself over to someone else and trusting them with the pieces.

Chapter 12

"Pleasure can coexist with awful degradation without meaning the degradation was justified or a species of wish fulfillment; how it feels to be both accomplice and victim; and how such ambivalences can live on in an adult sexual life." —Maggie Nelson, *The Argonauts*

I don't know how to talk about this yet.

Chapter 13

At a high school pep rally, cheerleaders and football players dressed up as class members who won the superlatives that year. Class clown, best dressed, most likely to succeed. They thought it was hilarious—the football players dressed up as the girls with stuffed bras and short skirts, and the cheerleaders in baggy jeans, popped collars, and baseball hats. Gender play at its school-sanctioned best.

I sat in the middle section of the bleachers with my friends and snickered. In the height of my early 2000's "punk rock/emo" phase, I rolled my eyes in my ripped-up jeans and spray-painted T-shirts. High school, for me, was shaped by the ever-present desire to escape it. Not from lack of friends or being bullying, but rather from an absolute certainty that I would suffocate to death if I didn't experience everything life had to offer before having children, which I assumed would put an end to actually living. I was a senior and highly motivated by the likelihood that I'd never see any of these people again.

When it came time to announce the class couple, the dynamic shifted. A popular football player stepped out in his jersey and faded jeans, fist pumping toward the crowd, as the gymnasium filled with laughter, shouting, and the stomping of bleachers into thunderous rumble. His fingers were clenched around a dog leash. Behind him, his girlfriend, a popular cheerleader, wore a dog collar, following him with a shy smile and her head slightly turned down. My classmates cheered all around me—

this was the first time two winners were playing themselves, and everyone knew what it meant. I scanned the crowd for teachers to see if any were looking as angry and horrified as I was. I didn't know the cheerleader personally; she was the kind of tall, gorgeous girl who was popular entirely for those reasons, though from what I could tell, she was also extremely nice to everyone. The football player, who had always been friendly toward me, was a regular proponent of freshman hazing and was rumored to be taking steroids. He paraded across the gym floor with his chest out, as she trailed behind. There wasn't a teacher in sight.

Six months later, the three of us moved to the same town two hours away to attend college. They were still together—one of those barely legal couples engaged before stepping foot on a college campus. He joined a fraternity, she joined a sorority. Rumors spread about what happened at parties. The things she did with and in front of him, presumably for him. Halfway through freshman year, they broke up. Sometimes I'd pass by her on campus, and she always looked happy, her cheeks pink, her UGGs salt-stained and wet, waving hello with a gloved hand, and her breath forming tiny clouds in the atmosphere around her.

Fifteen years later, I'm not sure if I remember any of this correctly. If maybe they did do the gender swap after all, or maybe she was the one pulling him on a leash, or maybe she was laughing the whole time, in on the joke, or maybe they didn't break up at all, or maybe nothing ever happened at those parties, or maybe rumors are really just rumors, or maybe, or maybe.

CHAPTER 14

I met Shane when he responded to an ad I posted on a Classifieds website. I was six months into my life in Tennessee, Christmas had come and gone, and aside from a few dates and random hookups, I had no real friends or support system in place. I wanted to meet someone, anyone, who could fill the void in my life for human connection. The best way to make this happen, I knew, was through sex. It was the only guarantee of someone being there when I wanted them. Over the years, I had begun to form a particular self-identity. An alter ego of sorts. I could be wild, a sexual force, a liberated woman whose freedom with sex and exploration set me apart from other women. Prude women. Women who weren't interesting, or exciting, or open to newness. Women who didn't allow hunger to drive their lives, like I did. I had given up the presumed love of my life, for a love of sex, I thought, so if it was not simply in my nature to think this way, what else was the explanation?

The ad I posted was funny and raw and erotic. Within 24 hours, I received hundreds of replies. Both amused and overwhelmed, I replied to a couple, but mostly just read them alone, in my apartment, laughing at the silliness of the whole thing. I had no intentions of really pursuing something, I realized. I honestly just needed to put something out there into the universe, express a want, dream a little of a sex life, an intellectual life, a romance blossoming out of something so crass that I would never again be rejected for all the need bubbling up inside of me.

Five days after I posted the ad, I had stopped reading the replies entirely. I couldn't keep up with them and what had started out funny began to depress me. So many of the men were married, or partnered. So many were significantly older than me, or younger, or degrading even in their initial contact. They didn't get my humor, they didn't get that it was about sex and wasn't about sex all at once. They didn't get me at all, and I felt foolish for expecting them to.

As I readied myself to delete the ad, I decided to open one last message. Immediately, I was taken aback by the length of it filling my laptop screen. After a witty introduction, the writer had taken it upon himself to go through my original post, line by line, and add commentary. He remarked on my sense of humor, how intelligent I seemed, how he too feels overwhelmed by his own ache for connection, how enticing my thoughts were, the ways he could relate to me, how compatible we seemed as people, how special and unique I sounded. At the end of the email, he revealed that while he checks off every box of what I was looking for—single, educated, professional, open-minded—there was one tiny hang up. He was 52, twice my age exactly.

I understand if it's a deal breaker, but please don't let it be.

Let's just meet one time. Then decide how you feel.

You owe it to both of us to give me a chance.

#

December 2017 – The counselor is warm. A teddy bear come to life. He wears a button-down shirt, light blue, maybe green, maybe yellow. He asks me what I hope to accomplish in therapy, and I say something about living. There is a ring on his finger that has probably always been there. A silver picture frame on his desk, light reflecting off the glass, probably a happy family. There are diplomas on his wall, a stress ball on the table next to me.

I wonder how long that ring has been there. I wonder when he became a doctor and what makes him trustworthy.

I want to work with a woman, I tell him.

Ok, he says, shifting. *Why do you think that is?*

#

During our first phone call, before we'd met, Shane asked me what I thought of cuddling, and I told him it was something that I reserved for the men I loved, which was to say, I would not be cuddling with him. He laughed, taken aback. That's not what I was searching for, I explained, leaving out that our age difference made our prospects slim to none, anyway. Besides, it felt fraudulent and overstated to pretend that the connection I sought with him would venture anywhere beyond our coital crawl toward one another through the emails and texts we'd exchanged all week. I was loving our witty banter and his sexy, yet gentlemanly pursuit of me.

But the idea of him actually touching me freaked me out. I had never been with anyone older than Carl. Anyone more than six years older than me.

Later in the call, we talked about sexual safety and birth control. I told Shane that I was on the pill, and when he asked why, I said because I only want to risk pregnancy or have kids *with someone I want to be with.* I said it flippantly because that's what it was to me—a casual remark about the significance of my own autonomy in the face of casual sex—a greater calculated risk for women than men, by far. But Shane didn't take it that way. He laughed, acting shocked. He couldn't believe how rude I had been. To tell him so explicitly, so directly, that I did not and would not want to "be with" him. *You could have been a little nicer about it,* he said. I was confused. *Nicer about what?*

What should have been a passing remark quickly turned into a long conversation about why I had said something so hurtful. Though he was laughing, making light of it, I couldn't help but feel ambushed. What exactly had I said that was so wrong? He was a complete stranger, not a longtime partner I had been picking out children's names with. But at the time, in my pacifying state, I apologized, not quite sure what I was apologizing for, but knowing instinctively I didn't owe it to him. We both eventually laughed it off. But in the following weeks, he would reference the phrase *someone I want to be with* like a punchline for our whole relationship. Still, years later, I am working to decipher its meaning, not sure if the joke was on him or me.

#

October 2017 – *What's the wildest thing you've ever done?* He asked, his eyes hazy, mouth wet with interest.

I was on another date with the man from the bar. Each time we met, I told him it would just be dinner, or just be a movie, and every time we ended up back at his apartment or mine, clawing at one another, feral desire coursing between us, unrestrained. The evening would start off awkward, me high energy, flirtatious, my stomach churning with nervous excitement, and him cool, easygoing, with the kind of relaxed confidence only a stoner earning a doctorate could pull off. Over the course of each night, our conversations would grow increasingly intimate, and the longing to touch him, hold him, and know him would furrow inside of me, a small animal begging for scraps of such longing returned. At some point during our dinner out, or trip to the movies, his fingers would fall to my knee, grazing it in small circles, igniting something within me that I could hardly contain. By the time we were saying goodbye, he'd ask to come in, or invite me to his place, and it felt physically impossible to resist. As we kissed and touched, he would tell me in a slow, soft voice everything he thought about me that night, every reaction, internal desire, his own perpetual longing revealed. Our time together would last hours, sometimes days, and I felt consumed by him in a way I hadn't felt with anyone since Shane.

But between dates we talked sparingly, sometimes weeks passing, before I'd hear from him, and at times I felt like maybe I didn't exist, that I was a figment of both his and my own imagination. We'd run into one another on campus, and my cheeks would flush as I pretended to be cool and carefree, knowing that without fail, every time this happened he'd follow up later with a text, asking me on another date. Once we were together again, nothing was off limits as I ached to explore every possibility with him while he was still in my grasp.

I can tell you mine first, he said.

Okay, I smiled.

I once fingered a girl while her husband was driving. It was really hot.

How did that happen?

He smiled back. *He was into sharing her, I guess.*

Oh.

My stomach turned.

They invited me to have a threesome, he said. *But I felt weird being that close to another naked guy.*

I get that.

He stroked my cheek with his thumb, pulled me close, and kissed me.

Now your turn.

#

Two weeks after meeting Shane, we got snowed in together for four days in my tiny one-bedroom apartment. Until then, we had spent all day, every day texting one another, to the point that it was difficult for me to get work done, or find time to make myself dinner. We were talking on the phone every couple of days too, sometimes from the evening until the following morning. After our date at the Italian Restaurant, we met a few more times, mostly him driving the hour from Nashville to Clarksville to see me for a quick dinner and an evening at my apartment, talking and exploring our mounting physical relationship. As uncertain about him as I still was, my attraction to him was growing. From the intensity of his gaze, the form of his body so impressively fit, and the tempered control and confidence of his touch, I was beginning to surrender my doubt in favor of a powerful want for knowing him better.

On a Sunday evening, during one of our particularly long phone conversations, Shane revealed halfway through that he was actually driving and on his way to my apartment.

I won't stay the night, he promised. *I just had to see you again.*

An hour later, he was draped across my sofa, reading aloud the first 150 pages of my novel, stopping to remark on parts he liked, or reactions to the content. We were spiraling into long, drawn out conversations about the ethics of love and sex, human nature, and my skill as a writer, the latter a backdrop to his every remark about the work. He made me feel like a real writer who had something real to say and the talent to back it up. My cheeks hurt from laughing, watching him act out the dialogue, as only a one time stage actor could.

It was 2am when he asked if he could spend the night. I was reluctant. Not only had I not expected to see him at all that evening, his visit lacked any invitation. But I had work in the morning and was nervous about how fast things were moving with him, a man I knew I didn't want to be with long term, but whose intense interest in me, emotional depth, and sexual prowess was drawing me further in the more time we spent together.

I'll leave first thing in the morning.

In Tennessee, I had come to expect only frost and the occasional flurry icing over my windshield, at most, so I hadn't checked the weather. When we woke, snow was blanketing the world around us, effects of an undeniable winter storm. My phone lit up with notifications of the university closing and winter weather advisories from the governor, urging everyone to stay home. It was a state of emergency. We were officially snowed in together.

Four days passed in a blur of intense conversation about fantasies, first loves, and his son and my father, our tears shedding empathetically for one another. We danced in my living room to classic country records on vinyl, cooked vegetarian chili and baked black bean brownies, stayed up late, and slept in each morning. We had swirls of intense, all-consuming sex, the kind that made me really feel like *someone*. These four days together were like living inside of an independent film, or an off Broadway play, I thought. An older man, so wounded from his life, the loss of his son in divorce, surviving an abusive childhood at the hands of a violent father, connecting in a once in a lifetime kind of way with a twenty-something divorcee, whose own self-identity existed around the belief that no one would ever truly love her. And the snowstorm!

How iconic. How unexpected, I thought. I even took some notes while Shane slept, imagining how I'd recreate these days together in writing so that I could relive them over, and over again, when I was old, and bored, and no longer interesting.

By the time the snow was melting and the state was opening

back up, I had convinced myself this was it. The whole of our romance would be relegated to these four spectacular days, neat and tidy, like 100 pages of screenplay perfection. When he finally left, I kissed him hard in my doorway, blinking back the heat behind my eyes, wondering when, or if I'd see him again. It was all just too magical to continue, I thought.

He was just too magical.

#

I haven't done anything wild, I said, coyly. The man from the bar chuckled.

I don't believe that. I know what you're like.

Do you?

His hands roamed my body, and he kissed me.

I know exactly what you're like, he said. *Just tell me. What's the wildest thing –*

I don't know how to talk about this yet.

#

I just want you to consider it.

Six weeks together, every night, every weekend, texting all day long, talking until our throats ached, entangled until our bodies vibrated apart, exhausted. I felt swallowed by Shane, like every hurt I had ever felt, or loneliness I'd ever known had fallen away as quickly as our clothing had, in heaps on the floor around us. It was as if he was filling in the cracks of my broken life, cementing pieces of it, and me, back together, making me a whole person again, or possibly for the first time. He was giving me a sense of purpose, a drive to exist each day knowing how deeply I mattered to him, and drawing attention to just how much I didn't matter to anyone else before. I needed him.

Don't be so close-minded, Lena.

A month in, I told him that I loved him. Not in words, but indirectly, he said. He could just tell, he said. Something was shifting between us. It was obvious something inside of me was cracking open, waiting to be consumed by him.

It was when he told me over coffee and cake that he would never be able to love me or anyone again; he was just too broken. *It's not you,* he said. *It's someone else.* The woman before me. The woman who was just one in a long, terrible line of women who had slowly chiseled away his well-being and destroyed him. He couldn't call her by name, it was too painful, he said. So instead, he referred to her as "the entity." And however much "the entity" had ruined his life, he said firmly that he would always, always love her. Always more than me.

It was when he said this, his voice soft, and his eyes gentle, his face and body radiating kindness, like it pained him to admit this unmovable truth, that I began to cry. When all the foundation we had been building started to fissure. When I began to grow desperate and needy, when I started to fear his absence, when I started to look sad, more often than happy.

That's when he knew.

Wanting this doesn't mean I don't care about you.

He wasn't like any man I had ever known. His careful attention meant every word I spoke had to be perfect the first time, or else we'd spend *hours* dissecting why I said what, or how I said it, or what I really meant. It turned out that I was capable of being hurtful far more often than I realized. Also, I was not a great communicator. I was always misspeaking, always misunderstanding him, always confusing dates, times, memories, promises. I also had a problem with lying. He would help me with all of these things. He would make sure no leaf was ever unturned; I would always explain myself thoroughly and to his satisfaction. I would always respond to texts promptly, pick up the phone when he called, open my door when he showed up unannounced with presents, or just to say hello. He knew I was a good, appreciative woman, unlike the others, but it worried him that I didn't always act like it.

I just really need this, if we are going to be together. I need you to do this for me.

He said he couldn't survive another heartbreak. I needed to prove myself first. He said that I was a special kind of woman. It was obvious in the ad I wrote, how shamelessly I talked about sex in it. I was exactly the kind of woman he'd always wanted to meet. A woman who embodied sex, who was sex. I was exactly like him; we both had the same kind of sickness. He could see himself falling for me, maybe. He could see introducing me to his family. He could see me. He could see everything.

But only if you want to.

Chapter 15

There are stories we tell about ourselves. Most of the time, they are fiction.

#

January 2018 – It's our first session, or maybe our third, or fourth. The counselor has told me that working with a male therapist might help me get over my distrust of men. I feel like a shelter dog, coaxed into being a family pet. He might be right. However many sessions in, I have learned that this man has a wife and two kids. He is funny and pragmatic. Kind, but firm. He's been sick all winter, and I feel sorry for talking so much.

What are you worried about? the counselor asks. So, I tell him.

I worry you will judge me.

Why would I judge you? he asks.

There is snow outside. It's been snowing for years. I am crying now, but I'm hoping he doesn't notice.

Sex is really important to me, I say. His faces twitches into an amused grin.

That's pretty normal.

I stare out the window. There are things I need to say that I don't trust a man can really hear. I don't say this. Instead I say, I don't know how to talk about Shane.

Let's start there.

#

I was with an older man for a while. He was really into dominance.

Oh fuck, tell me about it, the man from the bar sighed, shifting excitedly beneath me.

I was straddling him now, both of us still fully clothed. The conversation had stopped and started throughout the evening, between pipe refills, slices of pizza, and swapping one DVD for another. *The Godfather II* was now playing in the background.

Well, it's kind of complicated. It wasn't always…

His mouth trembled as he watched me search for the words. I kissed him, a strategic move to hold off saying it just a moment longer.

It's kind of like your wild thing, I finally said. His eyes widened.

You mean, he liked to share you with other men?

Something like that, I said, fiddling with his collar button, averting my eyes.

That's so fucking hot, he said.

Yeah, I sighed. *It can be.*

Did you do it a lot? he asked, eyes flickering with interest as he began to touch me. I squirmed, uncomfortable.

I don't know.

I want to know everything, he said, unzipping his jeans. *Start from the beginning.*

#

It's been years and I still don't know how to talk about this. There are flashes of apartments, of hotel rooms, of parking lots.

There are flashes of my body and someone else's, and someone else's, and someone else's.

There are names I don't know, faces I've never seen, just friction, and friction, and friction.

There is Shane in the corner watching. There is Shane telling me to stop crying.

There are men trying to be kind.

There is Shane documenting everything.

There is me loving everything.

There is me standing in the shower, begging him not to make me.

There is begging him to forgive me.

There is calling myself an object.

There is *believing* I am an object.

There is Shane saying I almost love you.

There is Shane telling me I did it wrong.

There is me saying please let me stop.

There is Shane saying *you wanted this.*

There are men saying *I can't believe you do this.*

They are whispering *why do you do this?*

There is me kneeling in the apartment, in the hotel room, in the parking lot.

There is a camera roll filled with my body, my body, my body.

There is adrenaline.

There is pain in: everything.

There is Shane saying he'd never force me.

There is orgasm, orgasm, nothing.

There is me asking if he loves me.

There is Shane telling me I'm nothing.

There is my reflection watching and my body convulsing, my rib cage closing, a divide forming—at once believing that there is no love in sex, only violence. Somehow, I had hoped for belonging.

This is not an apology, but there is shame. I'm not sorry that I'm sorry.

My trauma is the wildest thing I've ever done.

Chapter 16

I'm learning how to talk about this.

CHAPTER 17

To say everything that happened with Shane was unwanted would be a lie. There were things I wanted to do and, in some ways, I felt like Shane gave me the opportunity to try things that I otherwise would have relegated only to fantasy. I found some freedom in our exploration, and there were moments of legitimate joy for me. But to say any of it was what I actually wanted would also be a lie. Through the first several months of our relationship, I asked Shane, repeatedly, if we could stop. But six months in, after I called a particular evening awesome, he asked if I could ever be satisfied in a monogamous relationship.

I don't know, I had said.

But I did know. It wasn't about monogamy vs. non-monogamy. It wasn't about vanilla vs. kink. My sexuality and sex positivity were not, and have never been, limited to by-the-books, heteronormative, "love making" that we see in Hallmark movies. I've always been drawn to the strange, unique, mind, body, and soul expanding aspects of sex and life in general. It was simply that I felt I had no choice in the matter.

It wasn't that Shane ever directly forced me with physical violence, or restraint, though multiple experiments with bondage blurred the lines of consent far beyond what I would now consider ethical sex. It was that Shane's kindness toward me, his emotional openness, and the care he offered were contingent upon my giving him everything he, or anyone else, any man he chose, wanted of me sexually. He would state repeatedly that he only was interested in my enthusiastic consent, but when I hesitated at all, he would scold and belittle me, threaten to leave me, or in some cases grow completely silent right in front of me, unwilling to speak at all until I gave in. Sometimes hours of silence, permeating the yellow walls of my home, filling the atmosphere with the heavy weight of his disappointment, anger, and even disgust with me, would only end if I muttered an unenthusiastic, *So, when do you want to do this?* It was that when I did finally give in, he was there for me, supporting me, encouraging me. Paying for my application to graduate school when I couldn't afford it, buying me an Appalachian Mountain Dulcimer when I wanted to learn to play. Listening to me like no one else had ever listened to me, opening my mind to new and incredible things through the guise of religion and spiritual growth, telling me how special and smart I was, how there was no one in the world like me, how I was funnier, sexier, deeper, more talented and intelligent than any other woman he knew.

It was that his love had a price.

It was that no amount of giving was enough.

#

Fall 2020: My current therapist says that I'm emotionless when I talk about Shane, or any number of the things in my life that have harmed me.

It's like you're giving me a report. Like you're not the one this happened to.

I tell her, I'm both ashamed and unashamed by the fact that it hurt me. Much of the time, I said yes to Shane, or at least, I didn't say no. Some of those times I was afraid of him. Some of those times I was sobbing, and he was fixing my makeup, readying me to meet someone new. Some of those times I meant it: *yes, we can do this. Yes, that might be fun. Yes, ok, I will.*

To say yes was to be worthy, to belong to someone, to fulfill my role, to be interesting. No was equivalent to failing, neglecting, being selfish.

But it's all these years later, and I can't have sex without crying.

#

Our relationship lasted from January 2015 until summer 2016. After five months of dating, he moved in with me. After seven months, we moved to Kentucky so that I could start graduate school. During the entire first year of our relationship, we did things multiple times a week that I don't know how to talk about, and sometimes even more. I was growing disembodied, seeing myself through a voyeur's eyes, unable to recognize who I used to be. I was exhausted all the time. I felt owned by him. Prostituted. Somehow, the more I gave, the more he asked for. When I finally told him that I was done with that forever, that I couldn't take it anymore, that I didn't want any other man to touch me, he told me, for the first time, that he loved me. I couldn't bring myself to say it back.

We ended, finally, after I went away for the summer to intern at an artist and writer's residency in Woodstock, NY. I had just completed the first year of my MFA. We left on difficult terms, our relationship toxicity infecting both of us, in one way or another. While I was gone, Shane stopped calling. He stopped texting or responding to my emails. The void within me expanded. In July, I hiked the mountain behind the artist's colony where I was staying. When I reached the top, I cried out in pain and desperation. Out loud, and alone, I prayed to God for a sign, and the wind lifted all around me, a swirl of leaves, pine, and understanding. It was over.

In August, when I came home, Shane had moved out. While I was gone, a friend and member of my graduate cohort moved into the apartment directly below mine. We had been looking forward to being neighbors and talked about it over the summer. It took two weeks for me to figure out what was happening. In the two months, I was gone, Shane had pursued my friend and started a relationship with her, and moved in with her before I returned. They lived there for an entire year, directly below me, in an apartment with the same layout as mine.

I spent that year raw and wild, the ghost of him literally echoing in the hallway outside of my apartment door. There was no escape. I couldn't leave without running into one of them, or fear I would see him, and feel his eyes look right through me, like I didn't exist. I could hear their laughter echoing through the floorboards. I was trapped in poetry workshops with someone writing poems about him—forced to give feedback on verses written about her tenderly watching him sleep, holding him deep into the night, cradled in the protective arms of a man who *only* wanted to love and save her. A man who would, eventually, introduce her to God, a Christian faith, and a new way of life entirely—no fucking, or whoring, required from what I could tell. I was trapped in my home with the man who had exploited and traumatized me beyond my understanding, even now. Every time I left the house, I thought I saw him. At home, I'd hear footsteps all around me and convince myself he was there, in my apartment, watching me somehow. I started having nightmares every night of the two of them watching someone kill me, of Shane raping me, of Shane having other men rape me, of the two of them laughing as I died in front of them, a broken-bodied lump of blood and bone. I felt dirty all the time. Wounded and ugly, as if every bad thing that had ever happened to me—Carl, Jerry, Jack—every abuse, every rape, every violation, all the sex I endured against my will, all the grunts, sweat, and smells of men had morphed together into an unstoppable force surging forward inside of me, threatening to unravel everything around me, threatening to expose me to the world. I feared everyone else could see it already. At the CVS checkout counter, the warm hazel eyes of a curly haired employee lingering a bit too long, *Does she know I'm a whore?* The flirtatious interaction with the handsome stranger at Starbucks, *Will he try to fuck me in the bathroom? Does he want to own me too?* The long meetings with professors, one-on-one conferences with first year writing students, *Don't they know I'm a monster?*

I was ravenous to cleanse myself of him.

Chapter 18

Spring 2017: I'm reading a memoir about rape, assigned by my professor. It's the third book that we've read this semester that talks about sexual violence. The year earlier in my first memoir class, I wrote about my rape, back when I thought there was only one thing to write about.

The book is *College Girl,* and it goes like this:

There is a girl, in college, who is attacked in the night by a man that has been stalking her. He breaks into her apartment, holds a knife to her throat, and rapes her violently, in her own bed. She spends the rest of the book, the rest of her life, seeking justice and understanding.

In class, a woman across the circle from me says:

I feel like she's just trying to sound like a victim. I can't relate to this voice at all.

At home, I am reeling.

Two years ago, I said out loud, for the first time, that I had been raped. I told Shane, and he believed me. The first person I had ever told.

Now, I am sitting in my apartment. It is Kentucky-cold outside, which means it's Pennsylvania-comfortable. I can't stop thinking about this college girl.

I invited him back to my apartment, I think. *He broke into hers.*

I can't stop thinking about this college girl

Most of the time I forget it even happened, I think. *It wasn't a big deal, anyway.*

I can't stop thinking about this

Maybe it wasn't anything. Maybe I'm trying to sound like a victim. Not like this college girl, who didn't do anything wrong. Not like me.

I can't stop thinking about

Carl on top of me on Christmas Eve, my body crushed in submission.

I can't stop thinking

Of Jack forcing love from my throat. Jack forcing my body open. Jack forcing.

I can't stop

Shane's face when he tells me I asked for this in the ad I posted. Shane telling me I'm a slut and a whore. Shane cradling my face and kissing my cheeks. Shane telling me I'm only good for fucking.

I can't, I can't, I can't

#

To say everything that happened with Shane was unwanted would be a lie. There are things Shane did to me that I may never share in writing. Specific incidents, like the others, that if I could manage to recall in grueling detail, I'm still not sure I would. I still don't have a way of talking about them.

That semester, reading *College Girl,* I was blown wide open. There was nothing about rape that made sense to me, nothing about sex or consent, that rang true. I began writing to figure it out. I wrote that I don't know how to talk about my 23rd birthday, so I'll talk about it like this, and wrote the most detailed account I could muster of Jerry raping me.

Back then, it was still almost impossible to say out loud that

I had been raped. Not only because of how much I blamed myself for that incident, but because the word rape was so linguistically powerful to me, and the emotional trauma from that incident didn't resonate nearly as much as the other things I had experienced. The things I truly never talked about with anyone, up until that point. The things that reminded me more of the rape in *College Girl* than the rape I had experienced all those years ago on my twenty-third birthday.

I continued writing, sharing drafts with my professor, instinctively including outside research as questions arose inside of me: What do we talk about when we talk about rape? What is the connection between love and consent? What *actually* happened to me? What role does shame play in understanding? Who is to blame for all this hurting?

Over the course of the semester, I wrote a thirty page manuscript I titled "Consent After Birth." Rereading it years later, I am both stunned and pained by the ways in which I talked about myself and my trauma. The entire essay could be boiled down to one key idea: that I was complicit in every bad thing that had ever happened to me. *That* is the thesis. *That* is the point.

Still, this essay marked a turning point for me. As I was readying to graduate from my Master's and heading off to begin my doctorate, I was consumed with a need to understand what had happened to me. In all the research that I did for the essay, I came upon so little that focused on sexual violence in romantic relationships, and I began to wonder if anyone studied it at all, or if my experiences were really that much of an anomaly. Maybe something about me was the problem. But the more I wrote, the more I realized that there was one consistent issue that made it feel impossible to accurately write about these experiences or find research talking about them: I didn't feel comfortable calling them sexual violence. Without the appropriate language, it was difficult to even know what search terms to use that would ultimately reveal work that resonated with my experiences. Why is it that these words, "rape" and "sexual assault," which are meant to represent an action, have ended up representing the context of the action as well? Why is the context, so often, more relevant to naming the action, than the action itself?

#

May 2017: I'm finishing my MFA with one final summer class and a thesis defense. There are only two months left until I finally move to Ohio—escape the former friend downstairs, the former lover—start anew, someone smart and capable in Ohio, someone studious and self-contained in Ohio. Someone else entirely in Ohio.

But most days, I am clawing out of my own skin, feral in the summer heat. I still haven't cleansed myself of him. I still smell him on my skin. I'm trying though. I meet other men. Men even older than Shane. One evening at a local hotel, the man I meet is over twice my age, but incredibly nervous, incredibly kind. We spend a lot of time talking and being nervous together. He doesn't understand me. I feel guilty that he's married, but I pretend that's not real. I start out playing a character, a young and glamorous mystery. We spend a few hours together, and he is kind to me the entire time, and I start to play myself. Afterward, I sit in the parking lot and cry under the lamplight. I cry with my fists clenched, beating against the steering wheel and sometimes my chest. I cry for this man, for his wife, for how old he felt against me, for how disembodied I feel every day, for how damaged I must be to end up here, for how foreign it feels to be treated with kindness; I cry for myself.

I sit there for a long time. I don't know how to come back

from this place where I've found myself. I know it won't work to continue temporarily suspending my own morality to fill the need I have to wash someone else away from me. But nothing matters, I think. In the grand scheme of life, none of this matters. His marriage, my trauma. It's all stories to tell someone, someday. It's all entertainment as I watch myself disassociate. I can be someone else in Kentucky. Someone who doesn't care about anything.

I spend the summer in a full-fledged affair with this man, and when he tells me he loves me, I feel both sad and angry, knowing he doesn't, knowing he couldn't, knowing he only ever met a very small part of me. The part everyone meets: the brightness and the sun. Before I move away, he builds me a desk that I take with me to Ohio.

In Ohio, I try to be someone different. I post ads and delete them; I don't meet men that way anymore. I stop using sex as a costume. I don't want to be a body. But I meet a man at a bar, and he dresses me back up, plays make believe with me. I want to be something other than desperate. I know I am dirty, broken, and undeserving. I start my PhD program and wonder how anyone can look at me. I teach my classes and wonder if there's anything to be learned here. I don't feel anything in color anymore. On the phone with my mother, I call this peace.

I start therapy in December.

Chapter 19

The first time I ever spoke openly about rape, aside from with close friends and partners, was when I first announced to my PhD cohort and professors that I wanted to write a dissertation about sexual violence that would include outside research as well as memoir. I can't describe how strange it is to say this out loud to a group of people who you are supposed to have a professional relationship with. No matter how academically you put it—autoethnography, auto-criticism, creative-critical hybrid—when you say this, you are outing yourself as someone who has been raped. You watch their faces—some furrowed in compassion, others nodding knowingly (not necessarily from their own experiences, but from familiarity with the concept), others completely unmoving, afraid to make the wrong expression. You wonder what exactly they think it means when you say this. You wonder what they are picturing, and if they knew the circumstances of your experiences, would their faces morph instead into some kind of judgment? You wonder why no one ever asks you what happened.

I am still in the process of accepting that there is no right or wrong way to talk about individual experiences with sexual trauma. My approach over the years has been to either:

1) completely ignore that it happened, glossing over that part of whatever story I am telling,

2) to make light of it and comfort the people I tell to ease their burden of knowing, assuming the pain it caused me will

evaporate the more I laugh about it,

3) to eroticize it, or

4) to be so ashamed of it, I take total ownership for it, barely even acknowledging the other person's part in it.

While these are all ineffective when it comes to convincing others of the wrongness of sexual violence, they are not inherently wrong either. Each one is a layer of my own processing come to life. They are not true representations of what happened, but they are not necessarily false either. They are part of the narrative in my steps toward understanding what it means to be both victim and survivor.

I don't know that there is any such thing as a fully processed rape narrative, most especially when the context of the violence is inconsistent with what we have come to expect from that word. Something I have learned through all this is that, while there are definitely objective truths about sexual violence, such as this person forced this person to________, there are also subjective realities for the people involved that are equally compelling sources for understanding how sexual violence is perpetrated, and why it will likely never, completely, go away.

In all my subjective realities, I was the one to blame—either for not protesting loudly enough or strongly enough, for "allowing" myself to be coerced and abused, or perhaps most profoundly, for not ending the relationships soon enough—until I wasn't. It has taken me many years to accept this, and as with my relationship with Shane, and even with Jack, I still don't fully believe that both situations were not at least partially my fault. Which is why I struggle to analyze my experiences with them in the same semi-detached light that I could with Jerry or Carl. My subjective reality of those experiences has, over time, begun to align with a more objective reality of what happened. But, in so many ways, I am still working through the pieces of what has happened in my life from 2014 until now, and to present a fully processed narrative would be a lie. There is so much left to process. The best I can offer is fragments.

There are so many questions I'm still trying to find answers for.

#

So often, it feels like the women who speak and write about rape most publicly are those women who have an empowered understanding of what happened to them and their own survivorship. This is not something I relate to. More often than not, other women's abilities to openly and confidently name their experiences as rape make me feel one of two ways:

1) like I'm a weak woman for not being able to do the same, or

2) like I'm a liar when I try to.

Furthermore, it is nearly impossible to tell people you struggle with naming your experiences as rape, without them automatically, emphatically validating that it was. This may be a flaw in the contemporary anti-rape rhetoric. You can feel like a bad feminist if you don't loudly and vehemently call out any experience of unwanted sex as sexual violence, then end up blaming yourself for being weak-willed or a tool of the patriarchy. But the reality is, if we aren't active tools of the patriarchy, we are still products of it. The struggle with naming is never the fault of the victim, but the responsibility of doing so always is.

Naming an experience as rape, or even as assault, takes most victims months, or years, if not longer. The context of romantic love, and emotional abuse, if nothing else complicates this understanding, further distancing the language from the lived experience. In my effort to further understand the connections between romantic relationships and sexual violence, I followed through with my original intent for my research by building toward this memoir project, as much a personal journey of healing as it is a study of trauma. I wanted to know how, and why, it is normalized to be sexually violated, coerced, and raped in relationships that were meant to be beautiful and romantic. I wanted to know if "yes means yes" and "no means no" was really all that helpful when the line between yes and no is so often gray. I wanted to not only hear other women's stories, but pay careful attention to how they told them, why they chose those words, and what those choices meant in the context of American rape culture. But before I could examine anyone else, I had to examine myself.

While I don't believe all answers can be found in narrative, mine or anyone else's, I do believe the knowledge that exists inside of them is profound. The impact of language, the "rules" of communication, the rhetoric around sexual violence are all present in the lived experience, and the retelling of the story. In looking at my own retellings, the processed and the fragmented, it is clear to me now that language both helped me recognize and escape from the realities of what I was experiencing.

#

Fall 2020: Like everyone I know, I've spent months in relative isolation. Unlike everyone I know, I have also spent them in a near constant state of avoidance, finding whatever means necessary to escape the reality of writing a book I chose to write in the first place. Most of the time that I try, I'm afraid of what might come out. My therapist wants to know why.

There are two voices inside of me, I tell her. *One that tells me I'm lazy, and stupid, and incapable of doing it, and the other that tells me no one will care anyway, no one will ever read it, it won't make a difference, none of it was that bad, nothing matters.*

Neither of those voices are very compassionate, she says with a pained smile.

I don't know how to talk about compassion. Often, I feel like a victim of it, concerning myself so much with the needs and desires of other people, at some point I stop existing entirely. My therapist calls this over-identification.

Ramsey and Hoyt explain this through the lens of female objectification, the result of which is "to mentally divide [the female] body and mind in order to focus on her sexual body parts. Her body parts and their functions are no longer associated with her personality and emotions, but instead are seen as instruments to be used by others"… all of which increases the likelihood for sexual violence because, "it is considered easier to physically violate an object compared to a human…an objectified woman may consent to sexual behaviors that she otherwise would not, in part because she has internalized the view of herself as an object that exists to please her partner."

Film theorist Laura Mulvey writes that female film spectators inevitably internalize the "male gaze"—a term she coined in the 1970s, to explain this phenomenon in film.

> Traditionally, the woman displayed has functioned on two levels: as erotic objects for the characters within the screen story, and as erotic object for the spectator within the auditorium…She is isolated, glamorous, on display, sexualized. But as the narrative progresses she falls in love with the main male protagonist and becomes his property…by means of identification with him, through participation in his power, the spectator can indirectly possess her too.[1]

For Mulvey, women have two options when they internalize the male gaze: to over identify with the image of a woman as

[1] Mulvey, Laura. "Visual Pleasure and Narrative Cinema." 57-68. https://www.asu.edu/courses/fms504/total-readings/Mulveyvisualpleasure.pdf.

mere object, or to view women (and thus herself) from the man's point of view. It is no coincidence that this explanation mirrors Ramsey and Hoyt's research. Regular objectification and self-objectifications increase a woman's likelihood that she will see herself and her body through a "third-person" lens, thus disconnecting from the view of herself as owner of her own body. They also found that sexual objectification of women in media directly impacts male acceptance of non-consensual sex, in general, and within heterosexual relationships. The less women are recognized as human, the greater likelihood of sexual trauma both in and outside of relationships.

Is it possibly because it's painful to write about? My therapist asks me, her face kind. *What you're asking yourself to do is hard, especially because you're still processing what happened in the first place.*

I tell her that, sometimes, by talking about these things as if they hurt me, I feel that I'm calling myself a victim. *I don't want people to think, that I think that I'm a victim when at least some of it was my fault.*

But they did hurt you, she urges.

But I've hurt myself more, I think.

In *Come as You Are,* Dr. Emily Nagoski writes:

> Sometimes, too, survivors find themselves locked in a pattern of sexual behavior. Their brains become compulsive about undoing the trauma, redoing it differently, or simply understanding it. Like biting on a cold sore, or squeezing a pimple, the brain can't leave the trauma alone, even though you know you'd heal faster if you could. The result is that the survivor has multiple partners, often following a habitual pattern, without feeling perfectly in control of the decision to have those partners.

I used to think I knew which trauma I was trying to undo, redo differently, and understand. It felt obvious to me. My summer spent immersed in affairs I'm now ashamed of, convincing myself Shane was not to blame after all, that it was me the whole time, doing it all to myself. But then I trace back through the history, think it over, write through it all chapter after chapter, and I ask myself what if it all started much earlier than that.

What if I can trace my whole life back to Jack forcing himself on me in the middle of the night in 2014, or Jerry raping me the morning after my 23rd birthday in Tennessee, or the two male friends who, four months apart, touched me when they thought I was sleeping, and I was too shocked and scared to move, or Carl drunkenly shoving himself inside of me on Christmas Eve 2009, or my high school health textbook not including the clitoris in the drawing of the female anatomy, or men on the internet asking for underage pictures of my naked body, or the old man at the coffee shop where I worked in high school talking about wanting to touch my breasts between an order of sugar raised donuts and decaf, or when in the span of two weeks two different boys in two different classrooms whispered my name and flashed their penises at me when I looked their way, stroking while laughing at the look on my face, or seeing pornography for the first time BIGTITPOOLSIDEGANGBANGXXX, or not knowing I even had a clitoris until a stranger on the internet told me how to touch it, or hearing a dozen euphemisms for blow jobs before turning twelve years old but being embarrassed of the word pussy until my early twenties, or the male principal who measured the length of every fifth grade girls shorts after swim class to keep us from revealing too much of our pre-pubescent bodies, or last year, when at the Kroger check out, a woman came up to me and told me that she just saw a man I didn't know taking pictures of me, or the look on his face when I turned around and saw him, or how I cried in the parking lot afterward, barely able to breathe, feeling so reduced I couldn't look at myself in the rear view mirror, or how thirty five years ago, I was born a baby girl with bright blue eyes and a penchant for laughter.

Maybe this is all any of us need to know.

after
I went
I lived
I
chose to love
this list of stories

PART THREE

In Ohio There is a Window Always Open

and I want someone to notice
my skin sewn crooked from patches of light
I know women embarrassed to be naked in the presence of no one
no one a self they have selved into being
I know a man whose bones linger exposed
whose muscles tense when touched
I know a man I almost loved who loved
the color thighs shine when they creak open

maybe this is a poem about letting in
and out, maybe this is a poem about

before the earth grew moldy with people
there was a patch of bright expanding
I've been tangled in the rot of rivers
Run dry from exhaustion I've been
The river running from

No one
A self I've selved
A cage-heart I've settled into
Speak to me orange and I will burn down this mountain
Ember me lightning-lit and I will open

Chapter 20

Hi Lena,

Here are the notes from our session dated 6/28/23:

I woke up in the blue light of Pennsylvania, snow-hollowed and scraping.

Lena and I used the time today to talk about her experience of her trip

I got to Tennessee and I burned alive inside of it.

visiting places in which she experienced

Watched Kentucky turn me savage and brittle.

significant relational and sexual trauma.

In Ohio, I want someone to notice.

#

As I completed this project, I felt I needed to complete the story, too.

It was my plan to revisit every site of violence in my life.

Retrace the steps I took, the places where some part of me was made dead and buried, unearth it, scrape the dirt from its eyes, pinch its pale cheeks, and return it with grace to its proper place inside of me.

Try telling any writer that life doesn't require a narrative arc to have meaning, and watch her turn to stone before you. Acceptance without examination is like a dried-out carcass, bones so brittle and devoid of life, you could easily forget they were once animal, dressed in blood and muscle and fur. It is not life, and we are not human if our drive to understand this dissipates. We are the sum of our experiences, no matter how much we belittle or ignore them. No matter how hard we try to dress them up in new sets of skin.

#

6/28/23

Lena stated from the start, and several times,

I got to Tennessee and burned alive inside of it.

that it was a lot harder than she thought it would be.

#

To narrativize your own life can feel grotesque. Self-important and small. The self-focus can make you cringe. Is it authorial masturbation to divulge every ache, every pleasure, every violence? Is it delusional to see your own story as important and the miniscule details as wholly necessary to communicate that? Intellectually, I don't think so. I don't teach this way, either.

Your story matters!

All stories matter!

No one can tell your story like you can!

These are things I say with meaning and do truly believe, deep in the hollows of my bones. In one of my favorite TedTalks, which I love to share with first year writing students, Lidia Yuknavitch offers a brutal and beautiful testimony of how writing, claiming, and owning your life experiences can rebuild you.

"Tell the story only you know how to tell," she says, "Sometimes telling the story is the thing that saves your life."

No matter how many times I hear her say those words, they never fail to give me chills. The idea that we all have the capacity to rescue ourselves from the turmoil of what created us is profound to me. The idea that you can do this through the harnessing of language, whether in written form or simply in your own mind, means that we all carry within us the means to reinvention. I can't think of anything more empowering than this.

But when you begin to imagine your story as a narrative to be read, internalized, and understood by other people—that is, when you imagine the reality of publishing it—knowing that you cannot be there in their ear with a subtle footnote, or marginal comment, to revise it mid-read, update it to reflect your current state of thinking, or whatever recent revelation you had in therapy, or through some sleep paralysis nightmare, you can overthink the thing to death, and the powerful act of freeing yourself through words can feel like a broken promise you made to yourself. You know on some level your story, whatever it is, needs a universal meaning. An appeal to the reader. Something outside of you that grasps and clings to something inside of the imaginary "them."

It can't be *all* about you.

#

6/28/23

She was frustrated with herself

There is an ugliness in the gray and the waiting

that she could not find the words to express

for something meaningful to immerge.

what it is she needed.

#

I envisioned composing a final essay that marked the cyclical nature of my healing. It would be triumphant, I imagined, to return to each place where I experienced notable, identifiable violence or trauma, and write some sort of reflective piece on who I am now versus then, how I've changed, and what I've learned. While I never truly entertained the idea that such a trip would mark the end of my journey of healing, I gave the dream of this trip so much power. It will be so poetic, I thought, to come full circle and tie it all together with the narrative bow of returning, a warrior of my own battle. I envisioned a perfect and satisfying ending that would signal a finality to my search for understanding. It's not that I thought I'd have no *personal* work left to do, but I believed on some level that my "work" would be done, and I would put it all to rest. I would move on as a writer and person. I would close the book and only open it in reminiscence—a yearbook of human suffering, a nostalgic look back on the "before" of the after that would inevitably come, simultaneously consuming and freeing, but only after writing this final part.

Only after I completed the story.

#

6/28/23

As Lena detailed her trip chronologically

You could spend a lifetime running without ever moving.

it was clear that it was quite

In my case, I did both.
I moved,
moved,
moved.

re-traumatizing for her.

I want someone to notice.

Chapter 21

Allow me a timeline:

From 2017-2021, I researched the language of consent and relational sexual violence. In late 2019 and early 2020, I interviewed four women about their experiences, sat with them, silently cried with them, transcribed, dissected, and discerned meaning from them. In the quiet of my apartment, I agonized through each passing day, week, and month of 2020 as I, fingers suspended over my keyboard, felt incapable of generating quite literally anything to say about any of it. How could slicing through scar tissue, mine or someone else's, help anyone?

In August 2020, I embarked on the first leg of my "trauma trip," as I began to call it. I thought it would help me begin writing. Given the geographical distance these experiences crossed, it was impossible to do the entire thing chronologically. I would have to separate my experiences in Pennsylvania—my marriage to Carl and the Christmas Eve when he thrust himself inside of me, drunken lips pooling above with saliva and rage, the abuse and the fallout from my leaving, and the subsequent years spent in and out of love with others, before meeting Jack who betrayed my body, forced love from my throat, and made all of it seem normal—from the rest of it that took place in Kentucky and Tennessee.

This alone was complicated for me. I was already struggling with the nonlinear nature of how I first understood that I had been raped by anyone. In 2019, I wrote a poem with the line *I got to Tennessee and burned alive inside of it,* having spent years understanding my rape in Tennessee as the true beginning of my sexual trauma. But it wasn't, and returning to Pennsylvania forced me to confront that, directly. Although I had spent years, while living out of state, returning to Pennsylvania twice a year for holidays and a summer visit, each time I did so with an almost tangible revulsion in the pit of my stomach. Ohio was the only place that felt safe to me.

But these weren't the only challenges. Something else had irrevocably changed, and I was still learning how to live with it.

#

No subject.
Just *the body.*

4/24/20

Lena – It's Tony. Carl is dead. He died April 20th. Toxicology report hasn't come back yet. We are sorry for everything he ever did to you. It wasn't your fault. We are sorry he ruined your life.

I can't speak
overcome with illness
a marrow-level ache
shock and horror balloon
inside.

Carl is dead.

Everything stops.

I have no senses
no boundaries.
I am close to evaporating.

We are sorry for everything he ever did to you.

I am shaking,
heart racing, limbs tingling.
I somehow manage the words,
but I'm not sure what they mean.

We are sorry he ruined your life.

Sobbing deep and hard,
I think some part of me must be breaking.
This room is too small.
It cannot contain
the sounds of my wailing
and the news –

Carl is dead.

So I write, *I am so sorry for your loss.*
I am devastated. Then,

We are sorry for everything he ever did to you.

I forgave Carl.
I already forgave him,
and he knew it.

We are sorry he ruined your life.

He didn't ruin my life.

I am the only one left who knows.
Our story will die with me.

#

Very recently, in a conversation with my mother, she asked me if I ever really loved Carl. I was shocked by this question.

Of course I loved him, I said. *I married him!*

I know, she said. *But I thought maybe you married him just because.*

And then she sort of shrugged, like people do, when they don't entirely believe you, and it's not that serious.

But I was stunned by her asking me this, wondering how I could have given that impression at any point in my life, and if in fact I really had misrepresented my feelings for him, chalking it up to young love and poor choices.

When I found out Carl died in an email from his father, I spent weeks trying to discern the meaning of it all. Was it a validation, in some way, that I had made the right choice in leaving him when I did? Was he always destined to die at 37 years old, leave behind two children, and a lifetime of human potential? I recalled the comfort he found in Rodney Dangerfield, a comedy hero of his, who had only truly "made it" in his early 50s. There was an understanding within Carl, and me, that there would always be time. Time to recover, overcome, and succeed. But perhaps even I knew, back then, that his time was limited. That if I didn't leave him, he would surely leave me. The body being all that was left.

Though in maturity I have accepted that love wasn't the only reason I married Carl, and with experience, also recognize that we were not compatible in so many important ways, I can still say that without profound love, our marriage would have never happened at all. Although my love for him faded with time and distance as other loves dipped in and out of my life, I sincerely forgave him and only ever wanted him to find peace and happiness. The idea that he, his parents, or anyone might think that he "ruined my life" was horrifying. To say he ruined it would be to deny the entire life that I had built in the wake of him—the beauty and joy and tumult of it all. I was not only somewhat offended by this statement, but deeply sad. Did people just assume such an experience would break me irrevocably? Or had I done something to give that impression? I didn't think so. But I needed more than ever to reexamine my own telling of that story.

#

Summer 2020 – It is August and sunny and hard to explain to my mother why I must take a day, during my ten day stay at her new house where I am helping her get settled, to revisit places from my former life in Pennsylvania. Twenty minutes is all it will take to drive from her bright and beautiful new home to the one where she had lived so many years, including Christmas Eve 2009, as I stared silent at the snowy TV screen in her upstairs guest room, praying in quiet defeat.

What will you even do there? she asks.

Write, I say. *Reflect.*

Okay, she shrugs. Though my mother is a reader, artist, and intellectual, the practice of writing and the need to submerge oneself into the places and spaces that could inspire it is not something she necessarily understands. Or perhaps it's the lack of context that she is missing. The context I have not provided.

The content of the story she has never heard, but will appear in my manuscript somehow, someday. It is my plan to revisit every site of violence in my life. Retrace the steps I took, the places where some part of me was made dead and buried, unearth it, scrape the dirt from its eyes, pinch its pale cheeks, and return it with grace to its proper place inside of me.

This is the power of writing, I think. *I am an artist and a scholar. I will reclaim it all.*

I am truly this person.

Soon after I am driving, windows down, hurtling toward the house, where so much happened, and which sits on the edge of a town where I first sought freedom for myself, a young woman of only 21, radiant in my suffering. Though a short drive, in time, the road feels long with nothing but dark mountains, lush towering foliage, and the occasional respite of farmland to transport me. There is an anxious growth within me as my tires turn onto the dry dirt road of the address. My pace slows to a crawl as I pass small houses on my right, adorned with free-roaming cats and children, and the tumbling embankment to my left, leading to the shallow creek I once imagined bringing my own children to play in. The children I'd surely have with Carl. The children who could be in middle school, by now.

I press softly on the brakes as the car rolls past the front of the house. Repainted bright blue, more reminiscent of the house I grew up in than the one where so much died, not just for me, but for my mother too. A car appears behind me, so I drive further down the road past the expanse of the home's acreage, and park in the small rural church lot that sits at the edge of the property. The sky has dulled. A blanket of gray clouds has brought weight to the once sunny day, and sprinkles of rain scatter across my windshield.

I stare at the house. So far across the green. It is a beautiful house with a wrap-around porch and the kind of curved glass windows where one might imagine a Victorian widow soothed herself with the view of her expansive property and the nearby comfort of the church. For now, I don't know what I'm doing here. I cry, of course, and feel a little sick. My cursor blinks on my laptop, anticipating. So many memories, but they aren't just mine, and they aren't all bad. I write something: I recall, recall, remember.

Still, there is an ugliness in the gray and the waiting for something meaningful to emerge within me. I feel rotten inside and empty. So, that happened here, I think. *Who cares?*

I think, for the first time, that this was a mistake.

I reverse out of the church parking lot without looking back. Back on the dirt road, I drive away from the house and toward the town. Though my mother only moved from this place three years earlier, it feels like a completely different lifetime since I had last driven through the quaint downtown streets, with its old movie theater and gift shops. I am hurtling toward my next destination. She was not the only person who had kept an address here.

My old apartment building—a house with yellow siding and three units. I park on the street and stare at the downstairs unit that used to be mine, the slab of concrete before it now littered with tricycles and lawn chairs. My breath catches.

This was the first place I moved after I left Carl. Twenty one years old, soon to be twenty two. Memories flood, of course. I take out my laptop and begin to type:

Cooking alone. Starting to write my first novel. Never watching the paper-wrapped DVDs from my mail-in subscription to Netflix. The first man I had sex with after Carl. The many other men after him. I begin listing every man I have had sex with, in this apartment, and everywhere else, all irrelevant, and I recoil, my lips part and disgust escapes. This history is not mine, but then it is. *It is.*

I stop midway and page break.

Recall, recall, remember.

Within these walls, writing poetry feverishly, like an animal in heat. Joining the writing group at the local theater where I met, once a month, with retirees and the occasional twenty-something meandering their way through, like me. The old lady neighbor I didn't know who got locked outside of her apartment at midnight, who slept on my couch, and who I left snoring in my apartment the next morning when I went to work, who stole my bananas, and never said thank you. Four months sequestered in my bedroom during a year so poor and a winter so cold, I could see my breath in every room of my apartment, unable to afford heat anywhere beyond where I slept. The phone calls from Carl screaming in rage, wanting my address. The letters from Carl, begging me for forgiveness. The images of Carl parked outside, watching me, waiting for me, begging to come inside. The gnawing, aching loneliness of having to say no. Of wanting to be forgotten.

I left that apartment eleven months after I moved in.

Headed to the south. To somewhere new and beautiful. Somewhere I could be free.

#

It is August and sunny, and I am passing through another unknown, unglamorous small town where I had lived off and on during the two and a half years between my two separate moves to Tennessee. The town where I fell in love with Jay and fell out of it with Jack.

I stop briefly at my old apartment building—the one that

housed two of the three apartments I called home in this town. I park on the steep hill in front of the dentist's office, emergency brake activated and fighting for its life, and step out into the sunlight. For the next twenty minutes, I venture around the building, walking past old windows I once thrust open on sweltering summer nights, linger outside the door to the one Jack taught me how to break into using just a hotel keycard swiped from work, if I locked myself out someday. As I explored the outside of the building, knowing there was no way I could get closer to whatever was shut away inside, memories flooded me.

Those summer nights in such unbearable heat with no air conditioning, lying in bed, stripped down to my underwear, and sandwich bags filled with ice cubes perched on my feet. There were lips that tasted like wine and young men I wanted to love. There were lips like chapped ritual and the routine of wanting someone to be someone else. There were experiments in cooking—peeling two bushels of apples in my studio apartment and making homemade applesauce in a kitchen with a stove, a sink, and no countertop. There was writing in the downtown coffee shop and a date there with a PhD in Mathematics whose only personal interest involved repairing antique watches. There was the local bread shop where I bought a loaf every weekend from the shy and awkward baker and storeowner, no older than me, who gave me free croutons the more I smiled. There was the health food store that I couldn't afford but shopped at when the mood struck. There was the local library with its booths perfect for a full day of writing, and where my novel came into being. There was the downtown farmer's market where I befriended the fruit man with his organic peaches and cherries. There was the full spectrum of a life and so much living to remember, so much to hold onto. So much I didn't wish to forget.

I exit the town in a better mood than when I had arrived.

In both places I may have struggled, but I also lived my own independent life in the aftermath of Carl. Now I'm driving toward Scranton, where it all began. The final stop on my Pennsylvania journey. Memories abound as I pass through the city, to the "hill section" neighborhood where I lived my one year of marriage to Carl. I parallel park in a spot on the street, directly across from our old place.

It was not the first time I had returned to the apartment on Wheeler Avenue where we had lived together during our marriage. I had visited several times over the years, long after Carl and I divorced and both moved away. Once, in the middle of the night, I drove from another town just to sit in the car outside of that building and stare at the windows I once looked out of so hopelessly. Returning again didn't feel much different. It was surreal to gaze into the past and see myself there, young and unaware, standing in the doorframe, looking ahead. Almost as if I knew that someday I would return with distance and wisdom, wounded but free. I felt a longing within me to protect my former self, and yet, I didn't regret her either.

What changed was the feeling I had as I left. After spending time sitting on the street, staring at the apartment on Wheeler Avenue, my mother's old house, and the various apartments where I lived alone over the years, picking up the pieces of my life, I had a sense of exuberance. In so many ways, the trip felt like a reclamation of self and a cool, deep lake swim in the waters of my own resilience. In each of these places, I no longer saw a young woman, brutalized. I saw a young woman, unbreakable. I saw glimmers of the life that I had created in each place, moments of profound joy and heartache, evidence of my unrelenting determination to be happy despite everything, all the while constantly writing, always striving to build for myself a meaningful life. The entire region of my home state where I had come of age and propelled myself full throttle into adulthood felt like mine again, no longer weighted down by the heaviness of the trauma I experienced there, and the darkness I once felt had blanketed every square mile my pain had touched. I had reclaimed it for myself.

As I drove away, even the mountains and the trees looked different to me. Everything was beautiful again, finally, after too long of being gray and ugly. I drove with windows down and my hair whipping wildly through my car, music blasting, the sun shining in and around me. I was reawakened, some part of me returned to myself after too many years of letting it fester alone there, without me to love and nurture it. With this reclamation also came the validation that I was right in saying Carl had not ruined my life, but he had derailed it. As relieved and joyful as I felt driving away from these places, no longer afraid of them, I was at once deeply aware that what had happened between Carl and I was only for me to carry now. There would be no one else telling stories about it ever again. It would just be me, alone with the memory of us, forever.

It saddens me in some ways to know that to anyone else, the stories we tell about our lives are just stories, and the people we feature in them are just characters, so often absent of the arc. The stories, and how we tell them, get picked apart and used to represent whatever we need them to at whatever moment it is we decide to tell them. This doesn't mean any of it is untrue, but it might mean telling your story requires some depersonalization of the people involved. Excavating the ruins for useful, meaningful, entertaining bits to serve a higher purpose. But nothing is so simple as this. Carl was more than half of a short-lived, bad marriage, filled with violence and pain. I tried to capture that, when I wrote the early chapters of this book. But I'm not sure if I succeeded.

Part of survival is the demolition of all the ways in which the person who hurt you is more than the hurt they caused. It's a willingness to forget, altogether.

Chapter 22

It was my plan to revisit every site of violence in my life.

But, as always, I underestimated the emotional toll it would take to do any of this. This is a pattern of mine, which I find ironic. I am a person of silver linings and daydreams. I conceive of myself as such a bright and happy human that I rarely see the fissures before it's too late, and I am suddenly shattered. But I found that just the research and writing process was breaking me. I spent days and weeks writing in a fury, and then nothing for months. I felt trapped, suffocating under the weight of my own expectations of what I could and should be creating, and deep shame for it being *so fucking hard.*

The best dissertation is a done dissertation, I heard repeatedly, from mentors and colleagues. It didn't have to be artful and, most importantly, it didn't have to include a final narrative arc in the form of a travel essay meant to represent some conveniently timed healing process. So, in February of 2021, I completed a dissertation draft, a portion of which created the blueprint for this book, without embarking on my second leg of the "trauma trip." In March of 2021, I presented my dissertation research via Zoom to a panel of my faculty committee, doctoral colleagues, new husband, friends, family members, and even a few former high school acquaintances who decided to tune in. I was elated by this accomplishment. Though I was disappointed that I didn't fulfill my original vision for the project, I had overcome so much to reach that point. I presented my findings, smiled widely, washed down my victory with ravioli in rosé sauce and chocolate cake. I was victorious, finally. It was one of the best days of my life.

But the need to revisit those places lingered. I was drawn to the wet heat of Tennessee in the summertime, the blue sky glory of Kentucky where I had learned, and grown, and become. I didn't truly want to return to these places, but I felt that I needed to. I couldn't bear knowing there were places on this earth that felt off limits to me, specifically due to the fear of what happened there. When the opportunity arose to revise and publish this project, I had one condition.

I had to complete the story.

#

6/28/23

I shared my sense that her experience confirmed how difficult it is

I want someone to notice

for her to get close to those memories

my skin sewn crooked from patches of light.

#

From June 20th to June 27th 2023, I traveled from southeast Pennsylvania, where I now live, to Tennessee, Kentucky, and Ohio, in an effort to complete my trip and revisit every site of violence in my life.

In the month leading up to this trip, I cycled through various stages of denial and awareness of what it would accomplish and how it would affect me. My therapist of three years, who had early on diagnosed me with complex PTSD, and worked with me all throughout my original writing of this manuscript and beyond, questioned my reasoning for it. She warned of re-traumatization, of this entire experience doing more harm than good. I wouldn't hear it. I didn't want to. There were places I wanted and needed to return to and reclaim, just as I had in Pennsylvania three years earlier:

Murfreesboro, Tennessee—the city I moved after my divorce, and where I was raped the morning after my 23rd birthday.

Clarksville, Tennessee—the city I moved to where I eventually met Shane and the repeat violations from him, and other men, began.

Bowling Green, Kentucky—the city I moved to with Shane for graduate school. The same city where we broke up, and I struggled so much to survive his unyielding presence.

I would end my trip in Ohio where I had begun this work six years earlier and met Alex, the man who became my husband. Ohio was my safe haven. A place where nothing could hurt me.

This will be good, I told my therapist, as I planned out my route and booked hotels. I will travel through these places, see friends from my past, former faculty members, revisit places of deep meaning, and spend the summer finally writing the essay I always wanted.

But as the trip grew closer, I began to have doubts about going at all. I had started having nightmares, again, of the worst kinds of violence. I carried inside of me a constantly looming, directionless anxiety I could not understand.

What is your worst fear? she asked me during one of our sessions.

That I will see Shane, I told her. *That I will run into him in one of these places.*

What do you think would happen if you did?

I suddenly felt faint. Sick in my head. Sick in my core. Panic rose like vomit in my throat. I started shaking uncontrollably, crying almost hysterically.

I detailed to her my very worst fear—that I would run into Shane somewhere in Tennessee, in one of these towns on the outskirts of Nashville, where I know he now lives. I saw myself walking toward the checkout at Kroger and Shane appearing before me, having seen me across the store. Shock would course through me, an earthly tremor, and my body would petrify, turning cold and stiff, unmovable in his presence. My heartbeat would rise, deafening me, and whatever naïve sense of safety that I had found in the world would fall away, as our eyes locked and he took a hold of me, dug his long fingers into my brain and hijacked my very being.

Mind control? she asked, clarifying.

I didn't know what to say. I knew it sounded absurd. Humiliating even. To imagine this man who I had zero contact with in the last seven years could, in the very instant of seeing me again, puppeteer my mind and body so easily. It was a fear I wasn't even aware of. A fear I had never confronted or knew to anticipate. I was embarrassed about what I said, but I could not regain my composure, either. I was overwhelmingly afraid.

Though I knew the likelihood of encountering Shane there was extremely small, the fact that I could not completely rule out the possibility of it tortured me. In the following days, I finally revealed to Alex how I was feeling, and he also became concerned, not with me seeing Shane, but with how this trip might impact my mental health.

In the end, he agreed to go with me.

CHAPTER 23

We left on a Tuesday afternoon and drove until midnight, when we reached the halfway point between home and somewhere else. We stopped at a roadside hotel. In bed, Alex snored softly by my side as I watched, through the window, light shimmering across the wet of the parking lot, poetic and predictable in the darkness.

My eyes were open. They were open now.

#

6/28/23

She described a significant increase in PTSD symptoms that happened throughout the trip:

I got to Tennessee and burned alive inside of it.

Sleeplessness on the first night

In hotel rooms
I see
My reflection
In the mirror
In the bed
In the parking lot
I am haunted

#

We woke up in Virginia and suddenly: TENNESSEE.

Stopped at a famous gas station. Had barbeque and conversations about anything at all. As the sun and smoke of East Tennessee filtered away, the sky turned sallow, colorless. Clouds converged and suddenly: rain.

Exiting I-78, merging onto I-65 away from Nashville, signs for Murfreesboro, now just twenty miles away.

#

Physical symptoms:
Knee pain
Stomach pain
Shaking

#

The hotel was majestic with twelve stories, a fountain, and indoor garden sprawling like wealth and possibility. A ridiculously "hot deal" on whatever discount travel website. So unlike the first time I had visited this city, twelve years earlier, when I stayed in King's Motel for just $29 a night. My sister and I slept on top of the bed sheets with our shoes on and woke up stiff and aching from sleeping on a mattress as hard and creaky as a wooden floor. The next day, we met my soon-to-be Craigslist roommate and, for $150, bought a "new" mattress to be used once I moved, officially, three weeks later. Stopping for gas on the edge of town, and I said *people are so nice here.*

In the room, Alex spoke of dinner. But I was somewhere

else, fuzzy-brained and queasy.

Not sure what to do, or who I should be in this room in this town in this state so far from anywhere else I'd rather be.

I stared out the window.

He turned on his computer.

#

On the second night, avoidance of "going out"

Pelting rain and darkness
What do I remember but my own
bones breaking and
the streets where I died
a thousand times

(though she pushed through that)

#

I navigated the town without GPS, letting decade-old memory guide me toward the grocery stores where I once shopped, past the gym where an overzealous front desk worker tried to sell me on the promise that I could "fix" my pale skin with free tanning, included in the monthly membership. Past

WAFFLE HOUSE
WAFFLE HOUSE
WAFFLE HOUSE

on street names so familiar, like grade school classmates
you can't quite remember your impressions of. So much nothing, so little meaning. Four and a half months of my life
twelve years ago had resulted in this: driving dark streets

through rain and little recognition of much else, anxiety swelling and pooling in my center, searching for some part of my long lost self, when finally I arrived.

#

In front of the apartment I try to write
through windshield wipers
gently singing
you can leave this place.

#

The windshield wipers pumped. I stared at the building, much uglier than I remembered. I could still see my younger self, stepping through the entrance of the building and turning left, fumbling keys and pushing the apartment door open. The scent of hookah tobacco and weed. Bath and Body Works candles lit far too long. Step inside my bedroom BRIGHT ORANGE like a traffic cone or panic attack. I am so young here—heart and body-broken. Desperate to survive. Desperate to be seen and to be loved. Lonely in all the ways that loneliness can ravage you. Ravaged in all the ways that only lonely can survive.

This was my youth, but my eyes were open now. The wet heat of the parking lot penetrated like a bad dream. Somewhere, a car alarm sounded, and I startled to the point of tears, sobbing unhinged into the steering wheel. The night was dark, and the parking lot lit by only one lamp, flickering cliché cinema. I wanted to get out and explore the complex, but fear struck me. Oh, the irony of returning to a site of my own rape, only to be raped again, I thought. This time would certainly be worse, I thought. This time it would undeniable, even to me.

Still, I stepped outside in the soupy drizzle and walked along the sidewalk to the entrance of the building. Inside, it smelled like cat piss and cigarettes. Was this always the case, with my youth and low expectations rendering it acceptable living conditions? Probably. But my memory of it was different. I stood in front of the apartment door for only a second, before turning to exit, overwhelmed by the putrid scent. I walked across the parking lot to the small mail and laundry building, wondering why it matters at all that I retrace these steps. If I hadn't been raped here, would my memories of a mailbox and laundromat even generate enough interest to step outside, let alone walk across a wet parking lot, in the dark, alone at night?

I got back to my car and took a seat, staring at the apartment building once again.

This place was my youthful attempt at reclamation. Proof of my belief that anything is possible, and that the meaning of suffering will present itself to me, obvious and satisfying in its truthfulness. The belief that in Tennessee, I would find healing, and growth, and a love so pure and beautiful it would crack me open and free me. I am tired and sad for her.

Lena.

Only 22.

Just turned 23.

Lena so young and wanting.

So hopeful and trying.

Seeking shelter, but never finding it.

#

They whisper
You can leave this place
And I believe them

#

6/28/23

That night
"the worst nightmare" she has ever had

I lived on a mountain once
at the top where no one could see
the place or the man who had
confined me

that involved her being raped repeatedly

Cut open, threaded through
the violence of
knife and
dick
and dick
and dick

and no one believing her

They surrounded me
Teeth bared
Like wolverines

until finally she begged to be killed

some men imagine the ways

instead of raped

they might participate in your history of violation
one more time.

#

In the morning, the sky was bright, and I located the correct Waffle House from memory alone. Suddenly so obvious, so clear. Of course, this was the one. The large parking lot. The flat horizon destined for sunrise. There was nowhere else it could have been.

Is this what he intended for me when we met? Did he know that twelve years later, I'd be sitting in a parking lot, recalling every detail of a would-be forgotten and meaningless interaction if it weren't for the dangerous marriage of loneliness and politeness that influenced my next decision? I doubt it. I doubt he thinks about me at all.

But I've thought of Jerry many times over the years. Sometimes, I recall the color of his hair, or the details of his face that have not been lost to time. I think of his height. The thickness of his body, with a small pooch of belly not quite pronounced enough to hang over his jeans, and the overall mass of his form. I recall the complete desire that I had to leave his presence as we faced each other in the parking lot, the sun rising and casting a new glow across both of our faces. I wonder about his intention when he asked to come over just for a pre-work nap and why I'd ever trusted that would be it. I wonder if he saw my agreement as the act of compassion that I intended it to be, or an invitation for something I never suggested I wanted. I wonder if he ever saw me as a person, or simply a means to an end. *Spurt, spurt, like bad poetry.*[1] No condom. Only push, fuck, *rape.*

I could spend a lifetime contemplating all the wrong turns that I must have taken so that twelve years later, I'd be sitting in a Waffle House parking lot, seeking resolution. But I am not sure that I would find any. There was nothing else that could have happened. In the quiet of my car, watching the weekday crowd filter in and out of a Waffle House that sat inside so many of my darkest thoughts for so many years, I came to an important revelation. That I made the best choices that I could at the time with the knowledge I had of how the world worked and who would or would not hurt me. There was nowhere else I could have been. Nothing else I could have done. I was young, wounded, and a woman incapable of acting differently. From my position alone, it was inevitable.

In Murfreesboro, I remembered everything and nothing. Though some muscle memory of the city map remained, so much of it was unfamiliar. Like my return to those pivotal places in Pennsylvania three years earlier, there was an element of reclamation in this visit. It's not that I felt like Murfreesboro was mine again, but that I didn't need it to be. It no longer held the weight to me. Through returning to it, navigating the streets, sitting outside of my apartment where I had been raped, outside of the Waffle House where I had first met the man who was responsible, walking through the grocery store where I had once shopped, I realized how little of it I was still holding onto. I realized how much the memory of the place, and the story I was telling myself about what happened there, was part of what was harming me, now.

Through this visit, I recalled every aching detail of pain, loneliness, and hope I had felt about whatever "new life" that I had imagined for myself there. I embodied my own naïveté like

[1] Bret Easton Ellis. *The Rules of Attraction.* Simon & Schuster. 1987.

a pair of shoes I've long grown out of.

Murfreesboro, "the place I was raped the morning after my 23rd birthday." Such an annotation carries weight. But despite sickness and nightmares, painful memories, and revelations, this city meant nothing to me anymore. A blip in my existence. A stopover in the winding road of life. It is so easy to mythologize places for the wrong reasons. Trauma can do that to us. But it doesn't have to be the entire story.

Perhaps, instead: Murfreesboro, "the place I left behind."

CHAPTER 24

It takes an hour, through dark pine and countryside, to drive from Nashville to Clarksville, Tennessee. In the folklore of my own life, Clarksville had grown to represent my darkest moments. I moved there, alone, in the summer of 2014 and after five months of depressive isolation, met Shane. In my memory, it was the place that I never hoped to return to. The site of my greatest surrender.

#

4/28/23

She described a significant increase in PTSD symptoms:
Knee pain
Stomach pain
Shaking
Nightmares
Panic attacks
Crying
Numbness

In hotel rooms
I see
My reflection
In the mirror

In the bed
In the parking lot

#

But I didn't remember. I couldn't remember. Had I seen this room before today when I checked in with my husband, carrying my pillow from home under my arm, and a stuffed animal in my suitcase for comfort?

The whir of the elevator was so familiar. But aren't they all the same? Haven't they always been?

The hallways were so recognizable. But they all use that carpet, don't they?

The side entrance facing a field of dry grass and too much empty space.

In hotel rooms
I am haunted

In the bathroom, a panic attack. Dry heaves and dripping lips.

It was my plan to revisit every site of violence in my life. But, standing there, in the hotel room on the farthest edge of the city, I couldn't remember if this was one of them.

#

Since my earliest memories of beach vacations in the early 90s summers of my life, I have always loved staying in new places. Though there is nothing glamorous about a New Jersey shoreline motel with its leaky AC unit and carpet embedded with loose sand tracked in from the beach, there was an implicit excitement in stepping out of regular life and into the newness of another temporary one. Working at a hotel for a year and a half only solidified those feelings in me. I am the millennial traitor who just so happens to enjoy customer service, especially in hospitality, where the possibility of participating in someone's happy travel memories made me genuinely joyful about my job. But it wasn't just interacting with hotel guests that I loved. It was the entire setting of a hotel. The smell of cleaning products and air fresheners. The crispness of double-bleached laundry. The uniforms that we all wore as employees, which both anonymized and unified us. The delight in making people feel safe and clean and comfortable. The coziness of rain tapping against the glass windows that encircled the lobby. Little kids running through the halls with wet flipflops and towels wrapped around their tiny bodies, hair dripping chlorine and chaos. The poetic optimism of strangers from different cities, states, and countries, staying in the same place, under the same roof, sharing walls and continental breakfasts with one another, each entrusting their wellbeing to the several story building and hotel staff. I love it all.

So, when Shane first proposed we "expand our relationship" not only in my apartment, but nearby hotels, the thought soothed me. Beyond my genuine love of hotels, their inevitable transience has always served as a comfort. The depersonalized rooms, carbon copied, one after the other, decorated with soulless wall art and takeout menus featured in the guest book, only add to the anonymity adopted when stepping inside of one. *This is not my town. This is not my life. I don't exist outside of this space.*

Let's play pretend.

It's taken me years to consider whether this made it easier for Shane too. To depersonalize not only the space, but me, as I existed within it. It would be easier to forget my humanity when not surrounded by my artwork hanging on the walls, my favorite books stacked in piles on my bedside table, fairy lights strung strategically around the rooms indicating magic. Would it be harder, or easier, to hurt me with the photo of myself as a baby, happy in the arms of my siblings, plopped in front of an early 90s Christmas tree, perched on the top of my bookshelf?

I'll never know the answer to that, but I do know that bad things happened to me in both my apartment and hotels. But when you live in a place day after day, stewing in the site of your own abuse, you become numb to the backdrop. Revisiting hotels, I am only reminded now of the things that made me sob in the shower, stare at puffy red eyes and cheeks in the hotel mirror while Shane scolded me, or yelled at me, or refused to talk to me, after I had done something wrong. Maybe I was too nice to the man who he had invited there. Maybe I enjoyed it too much. Maybe I didn't enjoy it enough. Maybe I needed to do more. Maybe it was my fault that my body hurt. Maybe I was the one who asked for this.

The conformity of hotels makes it difficult, now, for me to ever feel entirely safe inside of one. Would it be harder, or easier, to hurt me in a place that I couldn't walk away from? The cookie cutter room layout remains the same in every city, state, and maybe country, so it's not difficult to step inside of one and flashback, like I'm flashing back to many years ago in Tennessee when I first accepted depersonalization—*dehumanization*— as a condition of my relationship. When I first felt afraid that who I pretended to be might one day become who I am.

#

Alex stayed behind as I drove away from the hotel to the city. Like Murfreesboro, I wanted to confront this place alone, fearful of what memories might emerge, and how it would feel to be struck by them in the presence of a man who loves but may not always understand me. The sheer normalcy of Alex's past intimidates me to this day. How can a man so well-adjusted truly love me? At times, I still struggle to trust it.

In that room, my anxiety reached an absolute peak for the trip up until that point. The distressing realization that I'd never be able to identify every location of certain violations and violences against my body, but I might accidentally stumble into one anyway, was suffocating me. I needed to get out.

Air conditioning on full blast, I drove sans GPS once again, allowing my memory to navigate the familiar streets through wet eyes and deep breaths. But the further I grew from the hotel, the anxiety gripping me like a tight fist began to release, and with that, my mood lifted. Visions of the year that I spent there came so easy and generously. Though I anticipated a horror reel of my first meeting with Shane, his manipulation and abuse, and the forceful way he took control of me, to obscure the entirety of my life there as it had at the time, and in all the years since I moved away, that was not the case at all. As I buzzed through the back roads of the city, passed the bowling alley where I'd participated in a weekly league, I couldn't help but smile. What a weird and random thing to do as a person with zero bowling skills or interest in gaining them. I approached the campus where I had worked, guiding myself by memory through the side streets that would lead to the tucked away gardens that I designed, planted, and cultivated all by myself. I parked, jumped out of my car momentarily, and grinned at the unbelievable growth that they'd had since I worked the twenty garden beds alone an entire summer in the Tennessee heat, learning about succession planting, composting, and organic alternatives to pesticides, via Google and 1970s gardening manuals. A student worker kneeled in the grass, weeding one of the beds, only looking up when my car door slammed closed as I sat back inside. I had thought about approaching her, telling her about the origin of the garden itself and how I had been the very first full-time employee hired to turn this space into something. I wanted to tell her about the times I had laid on the grass, covered in dirt and grime, staring at the sky. But these were my memories, and I was happy just to see them again.

I continued my journey through the city, parking briefly outside of the food pantry that I had managed for the university. So many hours spent packing, organizing, lifting, hauling, talking with students, shaking hands with donors. When I got the call that I'd been accepted to my MFA program, I was standing in the basement of that building. I picked up the phone, heard the voice of my soon-to-be faculty mentor, and stepped outside to scream into the darkening sky. As I drove through the beautiful downtown where I went to the farmer's market, past the soup kitchen where I'd volunteered on Thanksgiving, and the grocery store where I had shopped each week, Shane barely crossed my mind at all. All that came to me was the recognition of a fully lived life, work I was proud of, and the early signs that I was blossoming into someone smarter and more capable than I had previously thought. I felt like I had spent the last eight years suffering amnesia and finally regained my memory.

After my drive, I sat for hours at Riverside Park, on the concrete steps cushioned with strips of soft grass and watched the Cumberland River. Small children and their parents walked along the edge, fingers intertwined, hands swinging in the sun. In the five months that I lived in Clarksville before I met Shane, this was my ritual. After a workday, I'd head to the park where I spent most evenings settled comfortably on the steps with a book, or journal, or ukulele, surrounded by strangers but feeling a part of something. The wide expanse of water glinting in the sunlight before us, the blue sky just above, and the hope that I would find some meaning in my time there, however long, swelling within me.

In the late evening, I returned to the hotel. Though a faint pressure returned to my chest as I walked through the side entrance, rode the squeaking elevator to the third floor, and followed the patterned carpet to the door of our room, I was intoxicated with relief that I had not only survived my return to Clarksville, but truly reclaimed an important part of my own history, separate of Shane or any other man's impact.

Inside of our room, I held Alex, laid my head against his chest, and told him who I was.

CHAPTER 25

6/28/23
Lena felt she "reclaimed" two of the towns that have been characterized for her by trauma, in the sense that she could also recall good times and regain a sense of who she was there and her life there apart from the trauma.

I want someone to notice

my skin sewn crooked from patches of light.

Though her experiences in the first two towns were difficult –

I got to Tennessee and plucked flowers from the pavement.

Lena felt terrorized by her trip to Kentucky.

From a distance
it could have been any town in America
where no one can hear you
celebrate or scream.

She ultimately came to the conclusion

Kentucky turned me savage and brittle.

that there is nothing to reclaim there.

I know your real name.
I still remember your face.
I've memorized the shape.

Chapter 26

To narrativize your own life can feel grotesque, but to flesh out the details like a proper writer, can feel like scavenging your own dark, dewy remains. What stories do you want to tell, and what stories need to be told? Is the sound more important than its echo? I just don't know.

But I do know what I *don't* want to say, which is that explaining myself too much is like pulling a knife on an empty room. There is no one else here, and the sound of my voice is embarrassing. What is the purpose of this excavation, and will whatever I unearth leave an accurate impression? There is fear now, reader, that I haven't done my own story justice. That you'll come along with me to Kentucky and roll your eyes when I tell you how I was so terrified that I feared I might die there. That you'll point your thumb my way, voice dripping in contempt, *She thinks she had it so bad, but who is she? Who is she?*

Have you ever considered what sounds you would make if you thought no one was listening? I want to believe I would scream, but I am afraid I may only whimper. Does pain have to be loud to be dangerous? Cancer can metastasize an entire body before anyone thinks to look inside.

In the long process of recovery, I've asked myself how much my own silence is the problem. When friends told me, pre-trip, that such a return would be healing, that *there was so much good* and *being there will feel so much better than you think,* whose fault was it how wrong they were? Was it theirs for not noticing, or mine for whimpering when I had the chance to scream?

I want someone to notice.

How animal do you feel when covered in blood, and no one asks for details? I waited for my suffering to bloom bright enough for someone else to see it without needing an explanation. When finally, someone noticed without ever opening my mouth, it felt like God himself had chosen me, spread me open like sacrifice, communed in my bare center, a humble savior hollowing me for my own good.

By the time Shane noticed me, I had been waiting for years. He was lightning striking through a mountain side. But do you understand that, reader? Does it make sense without me adding more gruesome details? What more do you need to understand how a place, and a person, can turn you savage and brittle, forcing you to gnaw holes in your own skin for comfort? When the sound is gone, the echo is all that remains, and it stays.

It stays.

#

6/28/23

Lena felt terrorized by the trip to Kentucky.

I got sick at a roadside BBQ hut. My fingers hugged the bathroom doorknob, and I watched them tremble a nervous handshake.

At a Super 8 Hotel, half a mile closer to town, panic flooded my veins like poison. Paranoid and scared, I closed all the curtains, my full body under covers, my entire being—brain, joints, jaw, pores—radiating pain. I was either being torn open or sewn shut. I spent hours in silent darkness, in acute disrepair.

That evening, I entered the city as a complete stranger. I

lived two years in Kentucky, longer than anywhere in Tennessee, or any one town in Pennsylvania, and more recently than any of those places, yet I couldn't recall a single street. Almost nothing was familiar. No familiar landmarks, no recollections downloading in real time. Being there was more surreal than stepping inside of a dream, where even if there are no rules of gravity and your world flashes fluorescent chaos, everything still somehow makes sense. It was like exploring a city mapped by someone else's distorted retelling of memories you once shared with them. When you were young and trusted too easily.

She ultimately came to the conclusion that there was nothing to reclaim there.

Parked across the street from my old apartment, I was close to vomiting. Upon turning on the street itself, my body buzzed with panicked recognition. But to arrive in front of it, a building so dilapidated and ugly, it was hard to believe that I'd ever lived there. I was flooded with terror so thick and tangible that I could hardly breathe. Masquerading as just a house, at the top of a hill, in the center of a city in Kentucky where regular people live, this place was not only the place that I had suffered some of the worst pain of my life, but even many years later, it radiated a dark, psychic energy, that threatened to pull me in, and suffocate me in the process. It reminded me of the kind of portal to the underworld that you might find in an atmospheric horror movie. I knew the truth of this place, with its dirty white siding, overgrown lawn, and half hung shutters. Eight years later, it was still too raw, too recent, for me to be there.

She was not herself there. There was no self there.

My body convulsed violently. My teeth ached. My lungs were shallow and breath sharp. This was not only a place that I never wanted to return to, but it was also a place I actively feared, for the nightmarish possibility of being trapped there somehow. It was the site of Shane's greatest abuse. His manipulation, which felt like mind control. His grooming, which I mistook for love. His betrayal, living a full year directly below me with a woman that I'd once called a friend. It not only housed significant sexual and emotional abuse, but a spiritual death. Of all the things that I had endured until that point in my life, my relationship with Shane, the things he forced and coerced me into, and the eventual fallout which kept me imprisoned in the same space as him for a year, recreating my trauma on my own in deafening isolation, had permanently severed some part of my psyche. It changed my brain chemistry. It rendered me an entirely different person.

I don't know what provoked me to step out of my car, walk along the sidewalk, examine the front steps, and step through the threshold of the building. It seemed to exist in its own timeline. There was no one around. Just me, standing between four silent walls. My legs shook as I climbed the steps rapidly, almost running, catapulting myself to the second floor so I could stand in front of the door that was once mine. I brushed my fingertips against it, feeling the texture of the glossy chipped paint that separated me from the black hole behind it, calling to me in its own seductive whimper. As my skin made contact with the door, I could feel myself falling backwards, years of progress breaking away like rooftop shingles in a tornado. I could still access her. I could still feel her. The ghost of a ruined self, too tied to this place to ever be recovered.

I backed away from the door and drew a breath before escaping, quickly as I had come, down the stairs, through the lobby, and back into the humidity and the sunshine. If my biggest fear was being trapped there again, I wanted to believe I had proved it wrong. But something inside of me told me that I had not. I was still captive there. In some ways, I always would be.

Chapter 27

6/28/23

She is feeling at this time like she would like to avoid
the writing she intended to do as a result of this trip
at least for the moment

As writers it can be easy to hold onto a narrative far beyond its expiration date. Anyone can do this, really, but when writers do it, we can derail ourselves in a multitude of ways. It is not only a kind of limiting thinking that can disrupt your life progress, in general, but it's a restrictive trap that can smother creativity and expression. If you plan too much, try to dictate the profound meaning of a thing before you create it, make assumptions that there is something profound to even offer the world, you may risk blocking yourself off from the whole point of the experience to begin with. The significance is likely buried in the weeds, not blossoming in the daylight.

It took me almost a year of agonizing about this final section to even open a Word Document and begin typing. It took me a year of hesitation, extended deadlines, and the constant swirl of shame, and self-doubt, to accept that my desire to write this final section was not based in my humanity, but in my ego as a writer to give the reader a happy ending. But a happy ending is not always honest.

In returning to Kentucky, the illusion of a full circle narrative of survivorship and healing was broken. I drove away from my old apartment filled with a burning and bitter hatred for the entire city, state, and everyone that I met during my time there, whether deserved or not. I spat out loud my resentment, my fury. I passed the building where I had sat in every graduate class of my MFA program, where I taught my first classes, developed a plan for my future career, defended my thesis, and met the first true friends that I had in years. I had originally intended on stopping by and floating through the halls like a proud ghost. But instead, I felt nothing but disgust. I drove through the downtown, now all terribly familiar, and raged at the sight of the baseball stadium and the bright-eyed lovers holding hands, and friend groups falling all over each other in exaggerated amusement, roaming toward the ticket booth. These happy strangers represented everything I hated about Kentucky: at the lowest point of my life, everyone around me was celebrating. While I know this is objectively not true—that the personal struggles of so many of my closest friends in Kentucky made their time there challenging, too—feelings of neglect and pain rose within me, recalling so many nights spent alone, or surrounded by others, who seemed to access happiness so much more easily than I'd ever be able to, given the circumstances.

The truth is that I got to Kentucky and burned alive inside of it. I spent two years on fire, knowing the only thing that could extinguish it would be killing myself, or leaving. Because I couldn't leave without ruining my whole life, I embraced the only formula that I knew would help me survive—live as hard as possible and find every silver lining I could.

But in the summer of 2023, returning to Kentucky for the first time since I'd left it, I no longer needed or wanted silver linings. I had escaped this place once. I moved on, started over, rebuilt myself from the ground up, found the first healthy love of my life, got married, earned my PhD, and got a job as a college professor. I didn't need to turn Kentucky into something that it wasn't. I didn't need a positive spin, or to make it a safe place for myself to return someday. I never wanted to return, and there was no reason I'd ever have to. Sometimes, the best way to heal from trauma is to simply acknowledge the effect it had in the first place and stop trying to talk yourself out of taking it seriously. Sometimes, it is okay to say *this place can't be recovered. Let it burn. Let it burn to the ground without me.*

CHAPTER 28

6/28/23

I reminded Lena

I got to Kentucky and burned alive inside of it.

that, though it was important to her to return to these places

From a distance
It could have been any town in America
where no one flees
the fire inside.

the pain (then and now) was not caused by the place

I'll always remember
your real name.

but rather what happened there and the people who did those things to her.

I still know the lines of your face.
You linger in mine.

There is still a potential for "healing"

In Ohio there's a window always open

through additional trauma work

– a patch of bright expanding.

(not involving more exposure to place).

Maybe this is about
letting in and out.

CHAPTER 29

It took me a year to begin writing about my travel experience. Through that year, I assumed that as soon as I was ready for it, I would sit down, open a document, and the words would flow from me in ribbons. The hard part was over, I thought. I was safe at home, and I had things to say. Still, I spent eleven months in active avoidance, growing anxious with the more time that passed. Finally, when I determined I could not put it off any longer and still consider myself a writer, I sat down at my computer and looked for my document of notes. But, despite my laptop accompanying me at every location I visited during my trip, and my vivid memory of writing so much about each moment, the document where every note, every musing, every recovered memory and language-laced trauma response, did not exist.

Ever.

I spent hours, panicked, checking every folder, document, email account, flash drive, cloud server. It took a system-wide search of my laptop, using some programming black magic cast by Alex to discover that not only was the file nowhere to be found on my computer, no such file had ever been created, or saved on my computer, period. There were other files, work documents and photos, that I had saved during the same week of my travel, but not one contained the pages and pages that I had written about the experience itself. For the first time in my life as a writer, I had lost everything that I was relying on to begin. All I could do was cry.

It's like all evidence that this trip even happened is gone! I recall saying, exasperated and hopeless. I couldn't understand how this happened. I was insane with frustration.

Have you considered that maybe some part of you didn't want to keep it? My therapist asked a few days later in our weekly session. *Maybe you didn't want the evidence.*

The truth is that I had considered it. While I'm hardly an organized person, I have never lost writing before. Not since my days as a twelve year old would be novelist and floppy disc backups, anyway. It just didn't make sense that with all the time, effort, and emotional turmoil of embarking on this trip that I would be so careless as to lose, or somehow delete, the document. What made more sense was that something deeper was going on.

I couldn't stop thinking of what I had said a few days earlier—*It's like all evidence that this trip even happened is gone.* Was that true? Did the evidence only exist in the "gone but not forgotten" Word document? It couldn't. What would be the point of the trip if that were the case? It couldn't only be to gather notes for some ambiguous piece of writing. It had to be about more than that. It had to stem from something real.

Through tears, frustration, and resolution, I came to a fresh conclusion. The evidence of this trip *did* exist, but it wasn't in a folder on my desktop. It was in my evolution over the past year. In the ways I had grown, healed, and reevaluated my own life and experiences. But if there is anything that I've learned about myself in almost five years of therapy, it's that my ability to compartmentalize, turn parts of myself numb, and lock them up is a survival mechanism that becomes inconvenient when writing from a place of memory. I had a problem if I was going to write this essay with any of my original intent in mind.

Would you like me to read my notes from our session following the trip? My therapist offered. It may help trigger some memories.

Then I sat and listened as she read back to me the notes that she had taken, amounting to the most objective a recollection of my trip that I could possibly ask for:

6/28/23

Lena and I used the time today to talk about her experience of her trip over the course of the last week during which she visited the 3 towns in TN and KY in which she experienced significant relational and sexual trauma. Lena stated from the start and several times that it was a lot harder than she thought it would be and that she was surprised throughout in different ways about what she was experiencing. She was also frustrated with herself in that she could not find the words to express what it was she needed.

As Lena detailed her trip chronologically, it was clear that it was quite re-traumatizing for her. Though she felt she "re-claimed" two of the towns that have been characterized for her by trauma in the sense that she could also recall good times there and regain a sense of who she was there and her life there apart from the trauma, she also described a significant increase in PTSD symptoms that happened throughout the trip. She described sleeplessness on the first night, avoidance of "going out" (though she pushed through that), physical symptoms (knee pain, stomach aches, shaking), "the worst nightmare" she has ever had (that involved her being raped repeatedly, no one believing her, until finally she begged to be killed instead of raped), panic attacks, crying, numbness, bad feelings/mood, etc.

Though her experiences in the first two towns were difficult, Lena felt terrorized by her trip to Bowling Green. She ulti-

mately came to the conclusion that there is nothing to "reclaim" there. She was not herself there, there was no self there, just pain and suffering, which "flooded" her when she sat outside her old house where she was with ████ (from whom there was no escaping in that town at that time in her life). She also experienced panic at seeing white sedans during and for a while after this visit. This is the kind of car she associates with ████ and for a long time after their relationship felt anxiety when she would see this kind of car.

Lena became aware during this trip, but especially after the intense emotional response she had in Bowling Green, that numbness is her general response to periods of pain, and we talked about how when she started therapy when she got to Ohio this was her general state of being. Lena shared that the last couple of days of the trip felt good and Ohio (where she met and lived with Alex), "felt like a warm hug." As such, she has been feeling much better since her return and a decrease in symptoms. She is feeling at this time like she would like to avoid the writing she intended to do as a result of this trip, however, at least for the moment. She agreed that it would be useful for her to continue to talk about the trauma.

I reminded Lena that, though it was important to her to return to these places, the pain (then and now) was not caused by the place but rather what happened there and the people who did those things to her. I shared my sense that her experience on the trip confirmed how difficult it is for her to get close to those memories, though, there is still a potential for "healing" to come through additional trauma work (not involving more exposure to place).

In her reading, and eventually emailing, me a copy of her clinical notes, as well as granting permission to incorporate them into my work, I was able to recall countless intimate details of my trip, and through that, my own evolution. The fact that I had lost my own notes somehow felt like a blessing. I realized, now, that the only narrative I had to honor was mine. Mine. Me. The current self, a year older, with a year of marination. I couldn't have written it any sooner. I wouldn't have known what to say. Perhaps this, too, was inevitable.

Still, as I reach the end of this work, I fear making a final statement. I fear the final sentence I will write. How do you conclude a narrative that has no ending, but simply is? Any conclusion that I offer now may someday feel like a lie, and yet, the only truth that we possess at any given moment is whatever we've acquired by that time. At our most profound, we can only be a step below the version of us that will someday know better. It is possible that in five years, or ten years, or twenty five years, I will be someone entirely different. I will melt into a new self, who can contextualize life from an entirely new perspective. I can only hope for that. Because the one consistent truth that I have found about life is the dual importance of both understanding the context of what we have experienced, and what we think we know, and embrace the opportunity to revise our understanding of it. I don't particularly like the narrative of a happy ending, because it implies that someday the pursuit of it all will end. It marks a halt in evolution. I don't want to believe in any limits for myself, either in knowledge, or happiness, and I worry to treat this as a final statement on my understanding of gender, sex, violence, or even love, would be a betrayal of that belief.

So, I will simply say this.

I first titled this book *A Revisionist History of Loving Men* because it took me over thirty years to admit I'm still learning what love means, though I believe I'm getting closer. So, until then, I will revise until I've born a new language of stardust, and mildew, new words, and fresh sounds. Though I will never forget their real names, or their faces, I will continue to let in and out. Close and expand. Ignite and replenish. I will hold my own hand in the darkness, press lips against my palm, and embrace uncertainty like a man that I love completely. Because this is not an ending. When you turn the final page, you may hear it.

The soft sound of these pages –

pausing to take a breath.

Notes on Self-referenced Works

Each blackout poem featured throughout this manuscript originates from a chapbook-length collection of blackout poetry I composed entitled *Breathe Full/Burn Empty: A Separate History of Violation*. The original material used to construct this blackout poetry came from preparation for a qualitative research study I completed as part of my doctoral dissertation. For this project, I devised a list of interview questions to be asked in semi-structured interviews with my research participants. As part of my feminist methodology, prior to conducting my interviews I chose to answer each interview question myself, forcing me to directly contend with my own answers to these questions. From there, I composed distilled narratives of my experiences of sexual violence by blacking out or "erasing" the majority of words in each answer and honing in on the core reality of my experiences. The result is a collection of 20+ blackout poems—a few of which are featured in this book.

"Consent After Birth," which I quoted for an epigraph to Chapter 9, is the first essay I ever wrote, in earnest, about sexual abuse and violence. It was an essay born of raw heat, anger, and self-disgust. An essay in which I self-blamed and saw myself as complicit in all aspects of my own sexual trauma. While I stand by some of the ideas explored in this essay and am proud of the writing itself, with it being a finalist in 2018 for an award with Gold Line Press, I have chosen to never publish this piece for a few reasons. As important as this essay was in my journey toward truth and acceptance, it is also representative of so much internalized shame and self-blame, that I have feared it could trigger another woman in the wrong direction. This essay perfectly epitomizes why memoir can, sometimes, be a dangerous place to share your truth, especially when your truth must evolve for you to live. There is value in documenting the process of healing and discovery, but we must be cautious not to value our art over our humanity too often, or for too long. These things should co-exist without being a detriment to the other.

"In Ohio There is a Window Always Open" was originally published in *Dream Noir,* 2019.

Acknowledgements

I have been a writer my entire life and although I have occasionally shocked myself with the brutal truths that emerge in my work, there is no question that this is the most vulnerable writing I have ever done. There is something surreal and terrifying about revealing all your sad and ugly to the world, and yet, I close this manuscript today with a recognition of all the beauty that has emerged in its wake. I firmly believe that such work can only flourish in a supportive environment. Words, like individuals, have the power to move mountains, but the tectonic shift they generate is maximized when the power behind them is solid and unrelenting, which is to say, I have people I want to thank for making this thing possible.

I would like to first and foremost thank Autofocus, and Michael Wheaton specifically, for his support of this project from the very beginning. Through anxious phone calls, extended deadlines, and an evolving vision, you have been a supportive, compassionate editor, colleague, and friend. I am eternally grateful to you for giving this book a home with Autofocus, a press which exemplifies human bravery, vulnerability, and truth. Your open mind and kind spirit has brought me ease throughout this journey. You and your work represent the very best in independent publishing and I will forever admire your will and determination to publish books that elevate the unseen struggles that are so deeply connected to what it means to be human. Along this line,

I'd also like to thank Amy Wheaton for your beautiful cover design and your commitment to keeping the aesthetics of Autofocus reflective of the powerful nature of the books themselves.

I would like to thank the faculty members from my doctoral program who supported and guided me through the early drafts of this book including Dr. Lee Nickoson, Dr. Sue Carter Wood, and Dr. Daniel Bommarito. I am grateful for your belief in me and your grounding perspectives. I'd also like to extend my thank you to Dr. Dale Rigby who, unknowingly, supported me in my earliest attempts to confront sexual violence in my writing, who introduced me to creative/critical hybrid genres, and who told me that the word "patriarchy" was too simple and overused in descriptions of female oppression, which I took as the most direct advice to "show not tell" that I've ever received. You were the first man to hear my stories who didn't try to change them. Thank you.

Through all my life I have struggled with silence, with my burial of pain threatening to suffocate me from within. So, I would like to thank Dr. Jill Baird, my longtime therapist who for 5 years, and counting, has supported me in my struggle to speak, and challenged the narrative scripts I held onto too tightly for too long. Our work and your support have been instrumental to my healing, and my ability to do what I set out to do, both with this book and my life. You are incredible. Thank you.

Alex, it is like there has never been anyone else. My husband. My best friend. Everything has led to you. You've given me a home outside of myself. You have held me through this healing; you have taught me how to be loved. Not many men could be strong enough to love a woman through her hurt the way you have. To give space to my struggle and not make it about you. To ask for things, communicate, and give me space to love you back, fully and safely. Let's spend a lifetime. Why haven't we yet?

To Erin Slaughter, my sweet friend, you've held every one of my dirty secrets in your hands and loved me anyway. I love you forever.

To Allison Adams, a beacon of loyalty and strength. You have made me feel seen and known in all aspects. I love you eternally for all that you are.

To my parents, Michael and Susan, my stepmother Mary, my siblings, and all my core family who have brought me up from nothing, and always offer a place to land, I love you all dearly.

To the women I interviewed, whose stories may not be featured in this manuscript but were profoundly impactful in empowering me to tell my own story, I am so grateful for your bravery and vulnerability. You gave me strength, validation, and a driving purpose to continue in the face of every challenge.

Finally, I want to acknowledge every survivor of sexual violence who has ever come forward, for sharing your story. Your strength is awe inspiring. And for those who have not, and those who are still coming to terms with your own survivorship, you are not alone.

About the Author

Lena Ziegler is a multi-genre writer with a special interest in hybrid work. Her writing has appeared in *Split Lip Magazine, Indiana Review, Literary Orphans, Miracle Monocle, Duende, Dreap Pop Press, Anti-Heroin Chic, Gambling the Aisle,* and others, and she has been nominated for a Pushcart Prize. She is a co-founder of the literary journal and press The Hunger. She holds an MFA from Western Kentucky University and a PhD from Bowling Green State University. She is the host of the music and literature podcast *Reading Michael Jackson*, available on all major podcast platforms. She lives in Pennsylvania with her husband. She believes in magic, the transformative power of language, and resilience of the human heart. You can find her online at http://www.lenaziegler.com.

also from Autofocus Books

Duplex — Mike Nagel

XO — Sara Rauch

Until It Feels Right — Emily Costa

Cleave — Holly Pelesky

Nextdoor in Colonialtown — Ryan Rivas

Too Much Tongue — Adrienne Marie Barrios & Leigh Chadwick

Picture Window — Danny Caine

the nature machine! — Tyler Gillespie

A Kind of In-Between — Aaron Burch

How to Write a Novel: An Anthology of 20 Craft Essays About Writing, None of Which Ever Mention Writing — ed. Aaron Burch

Hiraeth — Mistie Watkins

That Spell — Tate N. Oquendo

My Modest Blindness — Russell Brakefield

A Calendar Is A Snakeskin — Kristine Langley Mahler

Culdesac — Mike Nagel

Razed by TV Sets — Jason McCall

In the Away Time — Kristen E. Nelson

The Body Is A Temporary Gathering Place — Andrew Bertaina

Daughterhood — Emily Adrian

A Healthy Interest in the Lives of Others — Teresa Carmody

Leave: A Postpartum Account — Shayne Terry

Yes I Am Human I Know You Were Wondering — Erin Dorney

Organic Matter — E.N. Couturier

Out There in the Dark — Katharine Coldiron

If I Can Be Honest: Selected Prose from the Four Years of Autofocus Lit (2020-2024) — ed. Michael Wheaton

www.ingramcontent.com/pod-product-compliance
Lightning Source LLC
LaVergne TN
LVHW091142080826
845145LV00008B/2232

* 9 7 8 1 9 5 7 3 9 2 4 1 7 *